TO LOVE, HONOR, AND VACUUM

When You Feel More Like a Maid
Than a Wife and Mother

REVISED AND EXPANDED

Sheila Wray Gregoire

Kregel
Publications

To Love, Honor, and Vacuum: When You Feel More Like a Maid Than a Wife and Mother, Revised and Expanded
© 2003, 2014 by Sheila Wray Gregoire

Published by Kregel Publications, a division of Kregel, Inc., 2450 Oak Industrial Drive NE, Grand Rapids, MI 49505.

Library of Congress Cataloging-in-Publication Data
Gregoire, Sheila Wray
    To love, honor, and vacuum : when you feel more like a maid than a wife and mother / Sheila Wray Gregoire.
    pages cm
Includes bibliographical references.
    1. Households—Religious aspects—Christianity. 2. Family—Religious aspects—Christianity. 3. Motherhood—Religious aspects—Christianity. 4. Time management—Religious aspects—Christianity. 5. Marriage—Religious aspects—Christianity. I. Title.
BV4526.3G74   2014   248.8'431—dc23   2014009326

ISBN 978-0-8254-4346-6

Printed in the United States of America
15 16 17 18 / 5 4 3 2

To Keith,
who vacuums better than I do!

Contents

Foreword

*M*y mother-in-law raised an amazing man.

From the very beginning of our marriage, my husband carried at least half of the household responsibilities. Our relationship has never been defined by "his job" or "her job," but by an "if it needs to be done, do it" approach. For example:

> When he's working out in the basement, he does laundry between sets.
> While I'm homeschooling the boys, I bake bread.
> Dishwasher needs emptying? He does it.
> Furniture needs to be moved? I'll give it my best shot with or without him.

We work together to make our house a home. It's the way it's always been, and it works well for us both.

That is, it worked until last winter, when my husband had unexpected ACL surgery.

It was the result of a moment of glory—while reliving his high school days in an alumni football game, taking the field in the green and gold of our alma mater one last time. Truth be told, he was a sight to behold. Watching him dive through the air and save a touchdown did wonders for our eleven-year-old marriage, reminding me of some of the reasons I was so attracted to him in the beginning. It helped me see my man through fresh eyes, and to appreciate his physical and mental determination to win. But midway through the second quarter, he hurt his knee, and what started out energizing our marriage ended up sucking the life out of me.

After he underwent an intense reconstructive surgery to fix an almost completely blown out ACL, I was left to take care of everything by myself.

My husband couldn't even get off the couch for the first few days post-op, so as I nursed and cared for him, I also had to maintain our home (clean, shop, do the budget, pay the bills, do the laundry), teach our boys, run my online ministry, take care of both our Labs, and meet a book deadline of my own.

I nearly lost my mind several times. "I can't get it all done. I can't get it all done. I can't get it all done . . ." were the words filling my heart and mind each day.

Stress levels ran high, children were pushed to the side so Daddy's more intense and immediate needs could be met, and I scrambled to keep our home presentable as friends and family brought meals to support us. I was so flustered by everything on my to-do list that I managed to forget a national radio-show interview—something totally out of character for me—and had to beg my publisher for a book deadline extension. In short, I was a mess.

Then, about two weeks after my husband's surgery, it began to snow.

And snow. And snow. And twenty-three inches later, completely snowed in and unable to do anything related to the outside world for several days, our family began to have fun. We laughed, dug a trench to our neighbors' house, and surrounded my husband as he hobbled over to share meals, play games, and throw snowballs. As the days went by, I began to see the good in all the bad.

Sometimes, what we call "bad" isn't really bad at all, but God's perfect plan to prepare us for His purpose.

I had chosen Psalm 92:4 to pray for our family that year, and God was answering my prayers right before my eyes.

"For you make me glad by your deeds, O Lord; I sing for joy at the works of your hands."

It came in the meals lovingly prepared by friends, in an unexpected opportunity to bless and serve my husband, in opportunities to teach my sons what real love looks like, and in simple evenings spent laughing as a family—the best medicine of all.

It's so easy to miss them—those moments of grace in the mess—but they happen most often in our homes. The place of our biggest to-do list can provide space for our greatest good. If we don't stop to look for the good, life and its massive, never-ending list of things to accomplish will suffocate us, stuffing down the gift of difficult times. But it doesn't have to be that way.

In *To Love, Honor, and Vacuum*, Sheila helps us see the gift in the mess and the purpose in the list. If you've struggled, like I have, to find the blessing of serving through your home, you're in the right place. Be prepared to look at your life through a whole new lens, and come out on the other side more grateful than ever before.

—Brooke McGlothlin
Cofounder of the MOB Society (for Mothers of Boys)
and author of *Praying for Boys*
February 2014

Preface

*D*iane is ready to snap. "Ted never lifts a finger!" she tells me. "He'll watch me struggle to get both kids in their snowsuits and out the door, and he'll just say, 'Can you keep it down? I'm trying to work.' He is always going out with his friends. But I have to ask permission to leave, and he hardly ever agrees. I'm just so tired. Every day, I clean up after them, I get dinner ready, I bathe the kids, I get them into bed, and I just want to collapse myself. But then he expects sex! How long do I have to put up with this?"

Laura is at a different stage in her life. When her four sons reached their teens, she decided to go back to work after being a stay-at-home mom for twenty years. She enjoys the work, loves her family very much, and appreciates their encouragement of her career. Yet their verbal encouragement has not been matched by any effort to help with managing the household. When she arrives home from work—usually after her sons arrive home from school—she is the one to start dinner. When her husband gets home, he disappears into the den and doesn't reappear until she puts food on the table. No one helps with the dishes, let alone with the vacuuming, mopping, and laundry. Laura finds herself as tired as she was when the boys were young, and resents the fact that her husband and sons still feel everything in the house is her job.

Little in this world is more tiring than being a wife and a mother. If you're a stay-at-home mom, you likely yearn for adult conversation and the chance to go to the bathroom in peace. If you also work outside the home, you could easily feel that you put in an extra eight-hour shift when you get home. And to make matters worse, there's often no end in sight because we think, "this is my job." You're poured out and exhausted, but this is the way it's supposed to be. That's what being a mom means.

As a Christian woman, that makes me sad. I feel like we're losing out on so much potential because we women are so tired! But then we seem to rub salt into the wound. Our solutions to women's exhaustion sound more like an admonition to "suck it up and get with the program" than a real acknowledgment that something isn't right. When it comes to housework, we ask, "Whose role is it to do it?" And if we decide it's ours, then the only solution is to buckle down and figure out how to do it better. It's as if our exhaustion and angst would disappear if we just learned to embrace our roles. And so many women do just that—they throw themselves into being a super stay-at-home mom, and yet the uneasiness, the restlessness, the doubt are all still there.

What if the problem is that we're asking the wrong questions? I don't think God actually cares who does the dishes nearly as much as He cares whether or not we're looking more and more like Christ. The issue to me is not, "Are you fulfilling your role as a wife and a mother?" but rather, "Is your family environment one where people actually learn to act like Jesus?" Personally, I believe being a mom is one of the most important roles we can have, and I believe building a strong family is one of our most important callings as women. But in emphasizing these roles, perhaps we've lost the bigger picture. The real question is not, "What should we do?" or "Who should do it?"; the real question should be, "Why are we doing what we're doing?" We emphasize form over substance, and that's where we often go astray.

Unfortunately, the message we so often get in Christian circles is, "If you just embraced your role, you'd find peace!" Then when we still feel exhausted and taken for granted, we think the problem is that we're selfish or not trying hard enough. We don't realize that maybe the route to peace was never going to be found in squeezing yourself into a mold in the first place. It only comes from asking God how to "do family" so that we all grow closer to Him.

And asking God how to do family is a pretty important issue—if not the main spiritual issue we face. After all, we spend two hours a week in church, but the bulk of our time is spent living as a family.

Which, in the end, do you think has more bearing on our kids' spiritual journeys, and on our spiritual life as a couple—those few hours in church, or our life at home? Getting right with God and finding peace is not about living up to an ideal of Superwoman, who manages to find the perfect organizing system to get everything done; it's about saying, "How can we, in everything we do, make sure that we reflect Christ and honor Him?" Since laundry and dishes and mopping take up so much of our time, and impact our emotional health, we can't separate them from what God may be trying to do in our lives.

Let's flesh this out a bit more. What are the repercussions if you are constantly overwhelmed with housework, children, and your other jobs while your husband doesn't seem burdened with his workload? Certainly it could mean you're physically and emotionally drained, but there may be more to it than that. If you feel like you work for your family, you may also feel taken for granted. And if you feel what you do isn't respected, you may also feel that you aren't respected. These feelings will affect your level of intimacy with your husband and your ability to raise your children well.

What are the repercussions for your kids if you throw yourself into being an awesome mom, paving the way for them to have a "great childhood," but you never expect anything from them in return? Creating a "perfect home" should have far less to do with being a Martha Stewart wannabe and far more to do with whether our children are on their way to becoming mature, responsible, independent adults.

No matter what your view on the role of women, I hope we can all agree on one thing: Jesus commended Mary for sitting at His feet and reprimanded Martha for being overly concerned with work. He did not say that Martha, who worried about preparations for a large meal, was concerned about things of no importance. Rather, He said that Mary had chosen what is better (see Luke 10:38–42). What is most important to Jesus is how we relate to Him. If there is anything hindering our relationship with Him, we are to "cut it off" (Matt. 5:30). We must allow God to structure our lives and our relationships so we are growing closer to Him.

So what does that look like from a more practical perspective? In some families it will mean mom does most of the housework. I certainly have for most of my marriage! But in other families it may not. That's why in this book, I'm not going to tell you who should do what. Instead, I'm going to help us wrestle through the far more fundamental questions: Why are we doing what we're doing? Is the way we do family helping people see Christ, or not? When we start to answer those questions, then it's easier to figure out what your family should actually look like.

In these pages I want to show you that by refocusing your priorities and changing the way you work, you can improve your situation even if your circumstances don't change. If you feel overwhelmed, I want to show you how to focus on what feeds your soul, rather than on all those things that sap your energy. And I want to show you how, when you make these changes, you can actually encourage your husband and kids in their spiritual life. Instead of smoothing life for them, you can take that journey of faith together.

It's been eleven years now since I originally put these thoughts on paper in the first edition of *To Love, Honor, and Vacuum*. Back then Polly Pockets, Play-Doh, and pink tutus were major parts of my life. Today it's Facebook, iPhones, and "Please, Mom, can you drive me to work?" My girls have grown into wonderful, independent teenagers.

I get more sleep today. I don't have crumbs all over the floor. Comparatively, I have oodles of time to myself. And yet I find that the same questions that plagued me then still whisper at the back of my mind: "Are you focusing on the right things? Are you too busy? Are you pointing your family to Christ?"

Those, to me, are the important questions, and if we can answer them in ways that fit our unique families, then the answers to who-should-do-what will naturally follow. But too many women in my circles didn't ask those questions. They just grew frustrated and tired and came to the end of their rope. Some decided to leave their marriages. Others didn't, but their lives seem so heavy. My prayer is that as you read this book, you will allow God to work in your life and your marriage. I pray He will enable you to find true joy in Him as He develops your relationships so that they're characterized by mutual respect, healthy interdependence, and true commitment to spiritual growth. If all of our families become places where Christian love is evident, and where we spur each other on to love and good works, instead of places where we try to live up to an impossible ideal, then the church will have found its most powerful weapon in transforming our culture.

Acknowledgments

It's been eleven years since the first edition of this book was published. Back then my children were barely in elementary school; today I'm almost an empty-nester. Life has changed. And just as my family life has changed, my professional life has grown. My blog has exploded; my writing has multiplied; and I speak all over North America now. I'm incredibly humbled.

So I just want to thank those who helped me on this journey. First, to my husband, Keith: for being the best husband in the world and always supporting my writing, thank you. You did a great job at holding off my recent nervous breakdown. You're awesome!

To my mom, Elizabeth Wray: I know I don't always talk about you that much in what I write, but know that everything I am able to do is only because you believed in me and gave me a great childhood. And it was a great childhood. Never doubt that.

To my agent, Chip, and my manager, Eric: it's fun having people who can tell me what to do and take some stress off of my shoulders. I appreciate you both!

To all my blog readers at To Love, Honor, and Vacuum: you have no idea how much you brighten my life. I hope I have even a small influence in yours.

To Fawn Weaver, Darlene Schacht, Courtney Joseph, Jennifer Smith, Julie Sibert, Julie Parker, and my other blog buddies: it's so amazing to be part of such a great online community.

And finally, to my guinea pigs, Becca and Katie: You have no idea how much I adore you. It's been the greatest privilege of my life to watch you both grow into lovely young women who love God. I'm so excited to see what He's going to do with you in the years to come.

Chapter 1

Diagnosis: Stress

*A*t any given time, we women are feeling guilty about something. I haven't called my mother lately. I let the children watch too much TV yesterday. I didn't serve all four food groups today. If you're not feeling guilty right now, I bet if you thought about it for a few minutes you could talk yourself into it.

Guys don't always understand this about us. They may think they've hit the marriage jackpot if they've mastered the sentence, "Whatever you want is fine with me, honey," but there are times when that's exactly the wrong thing to say.

If you ask your husband, "Do you think we should put Johnny in soccer this year?" and he replies, "Whatever you want is fine with me, honey," you're likely to want to bean him, because he just doesn't get it.

If Johnny signs up for soccer, someone is going to have to drive him. Someone is going to have to cart around those infernal canvas chairs with the soda holders. Someone will have to pack the cooler and then deal with all the dripping Popsicle mess. This is not a decision that can be taken lightly. And if he agrees that Johnny should play soccer, is he going to be the one to wipe up the Popsicle stains? Or is he volunteering you for the job? And if you don't want to wipe up the Popsicle stains—which is probably why you're going back and forth about the soccer decision in the first place—does that mean that you're a bad mother? Will you feel guilty the rest of your life because you've deprived Johnny of the Soccer Experience?

I once heard it said, "Motherhood is the guilt that keeps on giving," and I totally believe it. Whatever we do, we can never quite be good enough. And guilt can be magnified when women feel as if all parenting decisions are in our hands, because then the repercussions are also in our hands. We're the ones who will bear the blame if Johnny turns into a serial killer. So we overcompensate. We take on more and more of the parenting duties, because we desperately want our children to thrive. And in the process we may inadvertently crowd our husbands out, while driving ourselves to exhaustion.

A year after the birth of her son, my friend Rachel told me, "All I ever wanted was to get married and have a family. Now I'm a wife and a mother, but I'm so down all the time. At only twenty-three I've accomplished all I ever dreamed, and I'm so depressed." All her life she had been led to believe that having a family would meet all her needs. But when she finally had that family, she found herself overworked and empty.

Like Rachel, some of you may feel overwhelmed at your seemingly endless hours of work. You love being married, yet you feel frustrated because your busy life leaves no time for the other things you yearn to do. You're taking care of so many people, but who is taking care of you? You wonder why God would let you feel so drained when you have followed His will for marriage and motherhood. You have kept your end of the bargain, so where is the peace He promised?

Or maybe you feel like Brenda. Brenda has a wonderful marriage, and a fulfilling part-time job, but she never seems to have enough hours in the day to juggle the errands, her job, and all the kids' activities. Every night she goes to bed exhausted, reluctantly admitting to herself that it's not just the busyness that's sapping her energy; no one seems to appreciate anything she does. Her children throw tantrums, talk back to her, and never clean up their own messes. Her husband doesn't even notice anything is wrong. She thought family life was supposed to be peaceful, but peace is the last thing she feels.

Perhaps you're more like Diane, whose story I told in the preface to this book. You feel like you work from sunup to sundown, while your husband takes it all for granted. You do all the work while he gets all the benefits. You're tired and you resent it.

The Pressures Women Face

If you share any of these feelings, you're in good company. A recent comprehensive study on women's health found that women's biggest health concern wasn't breast cancer, or heart disease, or even their weight. It was much more mundane. We're all simply too tired.[1] And all too often we think the problem is inside us, rather than in what we're doing. To make matters worse, we tend to be more tired than our husbands. According to the 2010 National Health Interview Survey, in that critical 18–44 age group, women are twice as likely as men to report feeling exhausted.[2]

It used to be that the standard answer to "How are you doing?" was "Fine." Over the last decade that's morphed into "I'm just so busy!" We're all feeling pulled. Many of us, though, don't even realize there's something wrong. We're on the go so much, we start to feel like that's natural. Anesthesiologist Dr. Bradley Carpentier, who has studied the effects of exhaustion, explains, "We're now primed to be fatigued from the get-go. Kids are loaded with after-school activities; high schoolers are busy getting into college, where they'll only get up earlier and stay up later. Then come careers, the iPhones and BlackBerrys, the 24/7 multitasking."[3]

While Carpentier may think careers lead to exhaustion, I see that same frenzied pace whenever I speak at MOPS (Mothers of Preschoolers) groups. Most of the women I speak to are stay-at-home moms, but they're tired. I remember Lissa, whom I met when doing a tour of the Northeast. She had four kids under four, but she also was a MOPS leader, had her own at-home business, kept her house reasonably clean, and oversaw the kids' Christmas production. She wore her exhaustion like a badge of honor. "I'm always tired, but if you want something done, give it to a busy person, right?" she said with a laugh.

And here's where I get a little worried. I think this is actually a bigger problem for Christian women than for others. The North American church as a whole really pushes maintaining the traditional family, often in the *Leave It to Beaver* style. Let me be clear—I'm not criticizing stay-at-home moms. I have always been either a stay-at-home mom or, later, a work-at-home mom, and I love it! In most cases, I think having a parent at home is best for all concerned.

But often there are underlying assumptions about this ideal that really aren't that helpful. For instance, in this "June and Ward" arrangement, the mother typically meets the family's emotional, physical, and spiritual needs by keeping a warm, comfortable, and clean home, while the husband earns the livelihood. The responsibility for maintaining the marriage and raising the children thus falls upon the wife, leaving men relatively free to pursue their careers and other interests as long as they remain the figurehead "leading" the family.

Pouring yourself out completely for your family then becomes this Christian ideal for women. Deep down you probably know what I mean. Have you ever felt that if you admit to feeling overwhelmed, then you're rejecting God's will for your life? If you have, then you're dealing with a struggle shared by most of your sisters.

As more women pursue higher education, increasingly we're faced with even more agonizing decisions. If you do work outside the home, you're probably quite familiar with guilt. Guilt's a firm taskmaster, too. Guilt says, "The only reason you're so tired is because you've abandoned your family, so you had better work twice as hard to make sure your family doesn't suffer at all!" And so we try to do even more. Society's idea of a successful woman is one who has it all—a career, a husband, a family—and yet balances all the demands effortlessly. If the effortlessly part has always eluded you, chances are you haven't given up. You're just pushing yourself harder.

Work

What is it exactly that's tiring us out, though? Well, certainly women are working longer hours than men—though not significantly longer. A 2012 study by the Organization for Economic Cooperation and Development (OECD) found that American women's workday is twenty-one minutes longer than men's, if you add in both paid work and unpaid work.[4] I don't think those twenty-one minutes are really the root of the problem—though they do give men three extra hours of leisure time a week. I know many moms of preschoolers would give a lot for those extra three hours!

Nevertheless, I still think the real root of our exhaustion lies elsewhere, and a 2010 Pew study gives us a hint. On average, women do twice as much child care as men do, and men do twice as much paid work as women do. But women are twice as likely to rate child care as "very meaningful" as men are to rate their work as meaningful. And women are also twice as likely to rate child care as "very exhausting" as men are to rate their paid work as exhausting.[5] Therefore, women's work is both very exhausting and very meaningful, while men's paid work tends not to be either.

Let me put it another way: just like we've always thought, raising kids is the hardest job in the world. Yes, it's very meaningful, but it's also downright exhausting. And perhaps one of the reasons that it's so exhausting is because it's so meaningful. We're supposed to be enjoying it and cherishing every minute. We're supposed to know that the way we interact with our kids today will influence who they will grow to be tomorrow. This is crucial stuff. So when all we can think about is, *When can I get my next cup of coffee?*, the guilt hits again. If this is supposed to be so meaningful, why am I so stressed? The fact that we're tired makes us even more tired!

If our work as moms is meaningful, it means that we're emotionally invested. But you can't be emotionally invested 24/7 without wearing out. Men may work similar hours, but their work tends to give them a bit of a mental break. Women's work doesn't.

Obviously this is a generalization, since many men work in extremely stressful jobs. My husband, for instance, is a physician faced with life-and-death decisions on a regular basis. Playing the "Who is more stressed?" game isn't really a recipe for marital harmony. So the point of this research isn't to show you that you have it worse than your husband does; it's only to show you that, just like most women, you really do have a reason to feel exhausted.

Here's another element of that exhaustion: one of the roles that we take tends to be a managerial one. Just like that mom wondering about her son Johnny's soccer experience, we tend to be the "family managers." Men tend to spend the bulk of their child care hours playing with the children, while we tend to spend ours in physical tasks, like diaper changing and bathing, or in managerial tasks, like figuring out doctors' appointments or supervising homework.[6] Women are still the family's primary organizers. "Women are 'in charge' of running the house, while men 'help out,'" says Professor Marcella Thompson at the University of Arkansas in Lafayette. We tend to be the ones juggling all the family's balls in the air, trying to keep them aloft. No wonder we're tired!

In the fall of 2001, my family decided to take the plunge and begin homeschooling our two daughters, then ages four and six. Because my husband wanted to be involved, and I also wanted some time to write, he cut back his pediatric practice to three days a week. He taught the girls for two days, and I taught them for three. This was an ideal arrangement, one for which I was very grateful. But after two weeks of trying it, he remarked to me that he was finding it difficult coming home to a house that was so untidy. He could keep the house tidy when he was home; why couldn't I? I told him—rather frostily, I admit—that while he tidied up, he didn't do anything else. I took the dry cleaning in, did all the laundry, planned all the meals, cooked all the meals, did the cleaning, and ran all the errands. The only difference is that while I once had five days to do these things, I now only had three. I had a list of what went into running a house in my head, and he did not.

We've since written up lists of everything that needs to get done, and the house runs much more smoothly now. I still annoy him because I don't always tidy up, but I'm working on it. Most families, though, rarely come to such compromises, leaving the wife often very frustrated.

Men, of course, have not had an easy ride either over the last few decades. They're working harder, too. The New York–based Families and Work Institute reports that the average workweek has increased four hours in the last twenty years, to 47.1 hours.[7] And in many cases the work environment is much more toxic than it used to be. More work is being demanded from fewer employees. In the current economy, job security is almost nonexistent in many industries, so the pressure to succeed can be enormous. Increasingly, workers are being asked to sacrifice personal time for meetings, training, and other work-related functions, whether they want to or not.

Working women face many of these same pressures. In fact, pressure is probably the best word to describe what women feel. We're pressured at our jobs to work as many hours as we can; we're pressured at home to keep the perfect house; and we're pressured to raise godly kids, a difficult task these days. Our kids are growing up in a world saturated with sex, violence, and disrespect. Even teaching kids to obey is not an easy task. Every day, as we try to balance our schedules, our errands, and our enormous parenting responsibilities, we can feel the pressure building up.

There's no doubt that much of the pressure comes from maintaining our hectic schedules. A large part of it, though, seems to derive from the relationship patterns around the work we do, rather than from the work itself. When we feel responsible for everything—housework, child care, and everything that goes into managing a house—this can undermine our family relationships. Let's see how . . .

Exhaustion

First and foremost, women are physically exhausted. An anonymous mother from Austin, Texas, shared on the Internet some lessons she has learned while raising her children. Here are some of these treasures:

1. A king-size waterbed holds enough water to fill a 2,000-square-foot house four inches deep.
2. If you spray hair spray on dust bunnies and run over them with roller blades, they can ignite.
3. A three-year-old's voice is louder than two hundred adults in a crowded restaurant.
4. If you hook a dog leash over a ceiling fan, the motor is not strong enough to rotate a forty-two-pound boy wearing Batman underwear and a Superman cape. It is strong enough, however, to spread paint on all four walls of a twenty-by-twenty-foot room.
5. A six-year-old can start a fire with a flint rock even though a thirty-six-year-old man says people can only do it in the movies.
6. A magnifying glass can start a fire even on an overcast day.
7. Certain Legos will pass through the digestive tract of a four-year-old.

8. Superglue is forever.
9. No matter how much Jell-O you put in a swimming pool, you still can't walk on water.
10. Pool filters do not like Jell-O.
11. VCRs do not eject peanut butter and jelly sandwiches, even though TV commercials show that they do.
12. You probably do not want to know what that odor is.
13. Always look in the oven before you turn it on.
14. Plastic toys do not like ovens.
15. The fire department in Austin has a five-minute response time.[8]

I don't know about you, but if I had her children I think I'd be ready to snap. But we all have stories like these. I remember the time I found my children "helpfully" applying their own sunscreen—all over the chair, the dresser, the crib, and their clothes! But these mishaps, while funny in retrospect, are not usually the things that wear us out. It's the day-to-day caring for the children, looking after the house, and having to keep a million things straight in your head. It's hard to organize a house. It's so much more than just vacuuming. Housework guru Kathy Peel prefers the title "family manager," because it encompasses all that she does. And what she does do is very tiring.

Stress

Being a mother is hard. There's no one standing over you saying, "Wow, the way you vacuumed those stairs was inspirational. I have never seen anyone vacuum stairs as well as you can." No, when we're vacuuming stairs, washing dishes, throwing a load of laundry in the machine, or even talking on the phone, chances are little ones are pulling our pant legs, squabbling in the living room, or spilling paint on the floor.

When things are this difficult in other areas of our lives, we often give up on them. We tend to avoid things that make us exhausted. But kids are a different story.

No matter how tired or frustrated we are, I have yet to talk to a mother who regrets being home or raising kids. This gives a mom her greatest sense of satisfaction in life. In a large-scale study done by Focus on the Family in Canada, 86 percent of parents said their lives were better since having kids.[9] We love being moms. But on a day-to-day basis, there's little praise and a whole lot of hard work.

All of this is made worse by our culture, which assumes that kids will make us happy. The pinnacle of success for many women, as it was for my friend Rachel, was getting married and having kids. Motherhood, of course, can definitely bring happiness. But at 6:30 in the morning, when the baby is crying, the toddler is jumping on you, and your husband is storming through the closets because he can't find a clean shirt, "happy" may not be the first word that springs to mind.

"Stressed" is probably closer to the mark. Stressed, not only because we're wondering if we have enough energy to get through another day, but also because we're worried about what it means that we're not always happy in this role that was supposed to bring us bliss. In the process, we may try so hard to prove ourselves to others that we ignore our very real need for rejuvenation.

Harmful Coping Mechanisms

No one can sustain this behavior. Everyone needs an emotional outlet. And if we are dealing with pent-up frustrations, chances are that we have already adopted some coping mechanisms, many of which can actually make our situation worse.

First, when we are exhausted and struggling with the significance of our work, we may fill our head with mindless escapes. We spend hours on Facebook games, or scrolling through projects on Pinterest that we'll never complete. We become avid readers of romance novels, watchers of soap operas, and addicts of iPhones. Yet, because of their inherent emptiness, these activities can reinforce our negative feelings.

We can also turn to other things for comfort, and for too many of us, those other things are often found in our fridges. When we're home all day, it's all too easy to eat for pleasure, or even just to relieve boredom. One of my friends admits to hiding bags of cookies around the house, and sneaking off to munch on them where the kids wouldn't see. Not only did this affect her weight, she also felt extreme shame that she couldn't control her eating and embarrassment about being intimate with her husband. Others turn to even more harmful things: drugs, gambling—even online affairs. Anything to give them something else to think about other than how tired and lonely they feel.

The Decision to Change

Even though the picture painted so far is bleak, it can get brighter! We need to let God in. Too often we don't go to God with these sorts of problems because they seem mundane. We think God isn't interested in the day-to-day of our existence. Yet don't you think God cares deeply about the things that occupy the majority of our time? He's going to help you find a way through this exhaustion (1 Cor. 10:13).

If you picture this way in your mind, chances are you see yourself walking along a road, arriving at a fork, and needing to choose whether to turn to the right or the left. Robert Frost immortalized this type of decision with the line, "I chose the road less traveled by, and that has made all the difference."

While this sentiment is beautiful, I don't think change usually looks like that. I think it looks more like this: picture point A, the point where God wants our relationships to be. When we get married, we start our journey toward point A. We're not perfect, but we haven't had time to mess up that much yet! As we move along, though, we tend to travel away from point A. Unless we make a conscious decision to let God lead us to Himself, our human nature will tend to develop relationships contrary to His best will for us.

Thankfully, God doesn't take a hands-off approach. He orders our lives so that, in almost every encounter, we have the choice to continue along our old and tired road, where the scenery is predictable and familiar, or to travel along a difficult mountainous road back toward point A. The road looks intimidating, so we usually keep walking straight along our old road. Here's the problem: the longer we walk on it, the farther we're going to get from this point. God will continue to give us the chance to get back to point A, but as time goes on, getting back is more and more difficult.

Often we don't even see the chance to change unless we search for it. Change must be a deliberate act and can often be scary. Generally, it isn't something you happen upon, like a fork in the road, but something you have to initiate. Sometimes God gives us a nice kick in the pants to make us sit up and take notice, but it's quite possible for us to go through life with unsatisfying relationships that never grow any better.

The good news is that your family relationships can change, even if your family doesn't seem to want to. We have a God with great transforming power, abundant in grace and healing. So, how can you receive the help God can give?

The Foundations of Change

Some of you already place yourself squarely in the midst of your problems. Your husband is supportive, but you need some help organizing your life to better focus on what's most important. You may have an easier time with change because you've already put the onus on yourself.

Some of you will have a more difficult time because you think change involves your husband. He is the one making your life difficult; it's time the tables were turned. But change is not about taking away some of your husband's happiness so that you have more yourself. It's about you taking the bull by the horns to increase the level of happiness for both of you, so you can enjoy the kind of mutuality that God intended for your marriage. Sadly, some of us think that in marriage one person must lose for the other to gain. He's got that extra three hours of leisure time a week, and he had better cough it up! You may feel that he gets all the benefits while you have all the work. But change is not about reversing that equation.

No matter how it may feel, he does not have all the benefits, because if you are not happy, then he does not have you. Nothing in life is more satisfying than a marriage in which two people feel affirmed and accepted. If you find ways to increase your own peace of mind, that in and of itself will probably make him happier. He will sense the change in you, and that will change your relationship. And if he changes his attitudes and behaviors in response to your changes, your relationship can finally move to a place where you both feel fulfilled.

Ultimately your happiness does not depend on any change in your husband or children. It comes from taking responsibility for your own feelings, surrendering them to God, and then adopting new behaviors modeled after Jesus. The goal of this change is not an independence that makes your husband and children irrelevant. It is instead to become capable of managing your own emotions and actions, while allowing other people to bring out the best in you. You are capable of functioning on your own, but you will always function better if you are part of the team.

The church has long recognized the necessity of this sort of community. Paul, in 1 Corinthians 12, writes about how the body of Christ consists of many parts, all of them vital. In many self-help books, buzzwords like interdependence and synergy express the same idea.[10] Just like the Christian concept of community, interdependence is called the culmination of human relationships.

By its very nature, interdependence is two-way. Just as you require your husband, he requires you in order to live his life to the fullest. Now, many of you may stop here and say, "Well, of course he needs me! Without me he'd never eat. He'd lose his own head if I weren't here to take care of him!" This is not interdependence. When we say that he needs me "to do" something, we are saying that he needs a function performed, not a person to do it. If the only reason he needs you is to take care of the house, then he doesn't need you. Anybody could fit into that space.

But maybe that's how you feel. Many of the women we've discussed already feel that their husbands don't need them for their intellect or their emotions but only for their labor. Fostering interdependence means decreasing your family's reliance on you for what you do, and opening their eyes to their need of you because of who you are.

This process requires a change in us. We can never change another person; we can only change ourselves. As author Marilyn Ferguson states, "No one can persuade another to change. Each of us guards a gate of change that can only be opened from the inside. We cannot open the gate of another, either by argument or by emotional appeal."[11] We can pray for others, but we can only control our own thoughts and actions. We must first reevaluate our goals for our family to make them Christ-centered. Then we need to change our behavior to encourage these Christ-centered goals. Only then will we be able to say that our own happiness does not depend on our family but on ourselves and our relationship with God. With God's grace, we do have the power to change!

Meeting the God Who Changes Us

Some of you reading this book may relate to everything I've been saying—except perhaps the last few pages. You know what it is to be overworked, conflicted, taken for granted, or just plain tired. What you may not understand is how God has anything to do with solving these problems.

I believe He has everything to do with it. He loves each of us desperately and He wants us to have abundant life. But that life is not something He just gives us automatically. Instead, it's something we receive from Him when we begin a relationship with Him. Our lives will never be at peace until we are at peace with the One who made us, then redeemed us.

Let me explain how this works. God created people because He wants a relationship with us. He wants people to love, and He wants us to love and honor Him in return. God gave each of us the choice—it's up to us whether we want to have this relationship with Him. After all, the only way to know someone truly loves you is to allow him or her the freedom to leave. That's what God does. God promises He will walk with us. All we have to do is believe in Him and follow Him. But we usually choose to go our own way.

Even if you're a good person, you know what I mean. All of us are selfish, or lie, or are hurtful to others. God, though, never does any of these things, nor can He be around anyone who does (Isa. 59:2). Our wrongdoing—our sin—has to be punished, and that punishment is death, eternal separation from God (Rom. 6:23).

But this God who created us for relationship with Him can't stand this separation. He sent His Son, Jesus, to earth to die in our place. Jesus, who never did anything wrong, allowed Himself to be crucified. He took our punishment on Himself. He saved us from death by dying Himself. Through Jesus' sacrifice, God offers us the gift of salvation. All we have to do is believe Him. If we accept His gift, we become God's children and have eternal life.

But it doesn't stop there. God didn't send Jesus just to give us life with Him after our death. He wants a relationship with us now. God's Spirit comes to live inside us. He helps us to become more like Jesus. He will give us peace beyond understanding, if we let Him. That's what this book is about: letting Him change us so we can start to experience that abundant life. If you've never taken that step to start your relationship with God, I pray that you will now. Accept His gift. Read the gospel of Mark so you can meet this wonderful Jesus who loves you so dearly and who yearns to help you find peace. Then find a local church with other Christians who can help you follow Him fully.

Quick Reality Check

Are you chronically tired? Do you snap at the people you love? Decide today to trust God to lift your burdens. Read Jesus' promise in Matthew 11:28–30. Write it on an index card and place it where you'll see it frequently throughout the day. In no time at all, you'll have it memorized.

For Deeper Thought

1. Are you happy with the role you play in life? Do you think this is what God wants for you? Read Ephesians 2:10 and Psalm 139. God has a perfect plan for you. Ask Him to reveal it to you.

2. What's your attitude about change? Do you believe it is possible for your life, even in your current circumstances, to get better? Write out a prayer to God of what you want Him to help you change.

Chapter 2

One Step Forward,
Two Steps Back

The difficulty with change is knowing where to start. We feel bogged down by all the things we already have to take care of. But we women have always had to deal with these problems, haven't we? It's inevitable, isn't it?

Think about the mundane tasks that cause you the most grief. What things take up too much of your time, and leave you the most frustrated? Driving your children back and forth between karate classes, swimming lessons, and Boy Scouts? Taking your preschoolers to nursery school to make sure they get enough stimulation? Looking after all your investments and entering the statements into your computer? Doing stacks and stacks of laundry every week, let alone trying to find time to fold it? Picking up hundreds of Legos and ground-in bits of Play-Doh off of the floor?

All these things just seem part of being a good mother. Yet everything I've mentioned, without exception, is a new phenomenon in our culture, some new even within the last twenty years. We have bigger houses, more clothes, and more toys. Our kids are involved in more activities. Our lives are busier. In the next chapter we'll look at ways to save time on household tasks, but I really want you all to recognize two things first. Many of the issues we think women have always had to deal with have actually only come about recently. And the support we have had for our mothering tasks has steadily decreased at the same time.

More and more is demanded of us. Every day brings a new warning and a new crisis. A child's first three years are crucial, so you have to stimulate her. If he can't read by the time he enters kindergarten, he'll never catch up. If she falls into the wrong crowd in high school, she'll become a drug addict. You better make sure you're always sexy, with matching lacy underwear sets, because women everywhere are lying in wait to steal your man. Is this the way life has always been?

Let's look at three fictitious stories of women from different points in time, and see how the problems women have had to face have profoundly changed. If we put our efforts into historical perspective, we may find it easier to deal with our guilt and find better solutions to our exhaustion.

Meg, 1869

"Meg, wake up, honey. It's morning."

Meg heard the hint of impatience in her husband's voice as she rolled over and tried to grasp a few more seconds of sleep. The light was just starting to shine through the windows as she heard the rooster's crow.

"Come on, honey. Time to get Jacob up to do his chores." Meg sighed and heaved herself out of bed. She tensed, prepared for the cold, and wrapped herself in a blanket as she went to rouse Jacob. It was not a task she relished. He was his mother's son and was equally obstinate about getting up in the morning. As she opened his door, she heard the front one gently close as her husband, Paul, went out to tend to the animals.

"Jacob, time to get up." Meg nudged him and noticed with dismay that one of her nephew's army magazines was partially hidden beneath the bed. Why had Jacob borrowed that again?

Jacob was completely preoccupied by dreams of the army. Her nephew Jeremiah, nine years Jacob's senior, had secretly joined the Union forces in 1863. He had only been fifteen. Ever since he had returned, Jeremiah constantly told Jacob how much he had missed by being too young at the time of the war. Now all Jacob dreamed of was getting just a little bit older and running off himself. He planned to leave in just three years, when he turned fifteen, and volunteer to go conquer the West. In the meantime, he read all he could about soldiering.

"Jacob, I mean now. It's time to see to the cows. Now move." Jacob moaned and sat up, bleary eyed, as Meg left for the kitchen. As breakfast of pork and eggs cooked, she roused Samantha and sent her outside to tend to the chickens. Even though Jacob obviously yearned to be free from the farm, he was a hard worker. Samantha, on the other hand, was very scatterbrained. Meg often found her sitting among the chickens, talking to them, while they pecked at the sack trying to get at the feed.

Within an hour and a half, her two oldest were trudging off to school, leaving Meg home with the baby, Joseph, while she looked after the house. Paul had gone into town to check out the livestock for tomorrow's auction. It was a relatively quiet time of year, after harvest but before the big snows. Paul was busy planning for the next season, and today was out with his father and brother investigating the new calves being offered up. Meg prepared to start the big stew that would feed them for the next few days. Monday was cooking day, her favorite day of the week. Tomorrow, Tuesday, was laundry day, her least favorite day. Laundry was cold work as winter approached. Every Tuesday was the same—four dresses, six shirts, and three pairs of pants. She sighed as she remembered that Jacob would need new pants soon. She'd have to ask Paul to buy some fabric the next time he went into town.

She gathered turnips, carrots, and a few other vegetables from the cold room, and put them in the stew along with some fresh herbs, and beef from the cow Paul and his brother had slaughtered the night before. She glanced apprehensively at the new stove Paul had purchased for her after harvest. He said it was because she had worked so hard alongside him. She smiled, remembering. They had needed to get the crops in, but her brother-in-law had broken his ankle. So Meg had been outside with the men for over a week, working well into the night, while Grandma watched Joseph. It had been a lucrative year, too, unlike '67, when there had been so little rain that the harvest had barely been enough to get them through the winter. But this year had been wonderful. And she enjoyed working outdoors. As long as it wasn't the laundry.

The stove looked so lovely, but she still wasn't sure she trusted it. Her mother-in-law and sister-in-law had walked over from the family farm the day before to see it, obviously envious. At this moment Meg thought she'd like to give it to them. How did it work anyway? Caroline, her sister-in-law, accused Meg of hating progress. Maybe she was right.

Caroline had her own problems with her children. Jeremiah was still at home, helping with the farm, but showed no sign of growing up, despite his stint in the army. Even though he spoke glowingly of it to Jacob, Jeremiah often appeared troubled. Last week, when in town, Meg had seen her nephew dart into Pastor Peter's house after walking his younger sisters to school. Meg smiled, taking comfort in the fact that at least he was getting help from the appropriate place.

The day flew by as cooking days always did. Meg was delighted; the stove actually did work! She had managed to get ten good loaves out of it, and walked with Joseph over to her mother-in-law's house to proudly deliver one of them. It gave Joseph a chance to see his grandmother. And she sure coddled him!

Meg had looked around her husband's family homestead with a sigh. It was such a lovely, sturdy house, with beautiful furniture that Paul and his father had made together. "You mustn't be jealous, Meg," she told herself; yet part of her yearned for a house like that. Her own had only four rooms, one bedroom for her and Paul, one for the boys, and one for Samantha. And the rooms were so small. But they were her own. As she swept up before the kids arrived home, she knew she could take pride in the life she and Paul were building together.

She was startled out of her daydream by the sound of bells and horses coming up the lane. *That's odd*, Meg thought. Paul had returned an hour earlier, so it couldn't be him. "Who could that be?" Joseph ran out the door in excitement, and Meg followed. When she saw who it was, she stopped with a groan.

Mr. Latimer was holding her oldest son by the collar and looking grim. Jacob was scowling, with a fresh bruise swelling near his eye. What had he done now? Before she could say anything, Paul was running over from the barn.

"Hi, Tom. What have you got there?" While Meg felt embarrassed, Paul had a twinkle in his eye.

"I caught this one pummeling my Andrew, in front of the church, of all places! I gave Andrew a good swat for starting it, and then I thought I'd better drive this one home myself. Those two are always getting into trouble together."

"Thanks, Tom. I'll deal with him."

After Mr. Latimer left, Paul had a rather testy heart-to-heart with Jacob, who was now on double chores for the rest of the week. Paul didn't mind punishing him; after all, if Jacob did double chores, then Paul would get some time off! Whenever Meg suggested that their son had a serious problem, he laughed and told her that Jacob would grow out of it. After all, Paul had given his own father no end of trouble, he had told her. But as soon as he had laid eyes on Meg, all he could think about was settling down with her. He assured her Jacob would be the same way. Meg flushed as she remembered their late-night conversation. After their talk, Paul had worked hard to convince her he was right. She desperately hoped he was.

She'd take the family up to Caroline's tonight and pray about it with her. Caroline always knew what to say. Meg had another reason for wanting to go to Caroline's anyway. Samantha had spelled almost every word wrong on her test today. Meg couldn't understand it. She herself had always been such a good student. But Caroline had been a teacher before she had married and was wonderful with Samantha. She'd show Meg how to help Sam.

The family sat in awkward silence to eat their stew. Everybody was a little tense. Finally, Paul laughed. "Well, if we're going to sit here saying nothing, I may as well go back and tend to the cows. Joseph, why don't you tell me what you did today?" And as Joseph prattled on about Grandma's new puppies, Meg smiled. Despite her worries, it was lovely to have her family all together.

Valerie, 1952

Valerie glanced at Amy, corralled amidst a pile of cushions. She had just managed to get her settled with some building blocks before she had lugged out the vacuum. She hoped Amy would stay put. Her eighteen-month-old loved the sound of the vacuum and would often crawl in front of it for fun, making it very difficult to get anything done.

And Valerie had a lot to get done today. She had put a load of laundry in the washing machine this morning. The machine was new, with a spinner and a wringer built in, and was very convenient. Now she only had to do laundry two days a week because the machine was so much quicker. She wanted to get the vacuuming and dusting done in a hurry, so she could move on to the ironing before 10:30. It was Tuesday, and often on Tuesdays her sister and some friends would drop in for coffee with their toddlers.

She replaced some of the toys Amy had scattered on the floor, then lugged out the iron to start what was her least favorite task. Bill was very particular about his shirts. He couldn't understand why Valerie was so organized at some things but couldn't iron a shirt properly. She had tried, but she just wasn't as fussy as he was. It didn't seem worth the effort. So what if there were a few wrinkles under the arms? Bill would be wearing a suit jacket anyway.

Valerie sighed as she remembered the night before. They had stayed up late talking, even though Valerie wanted to sleep. Bill was upset about his job and wanted Valerie to listen to him. She did, but when she offered a suggestion—like perhaps he should go to his boss and ask directly for one of the new accounts—Bill interpreted it as Valerie not having faith in him. It wasn't that. She just felt Bill was too timid at work.

She had met Bill when they worked on the yearbook at college. Valerie had been the director of the yearbook committee, while Bill had organized the layout. She had loved the challenge and hoped that maybe she would be able to find something else she could sink her teeth into once Amy was in school. Maybe she could volunteer at the school and organize something there. Bill wouldn't object to that— she'd still be home in the evenings. And during the war Valerie had managed to organize a whole volunteer brigade at the veterans' hospital, while Bill worked in supplies. She had done her part, though it was awfully busy juggling her war work with making dinner. But she'd done it. Of course she was glad the war was over, but sometimes she missed those days of excitement, feeling like she was part of something more than just ironing a shirt.

Just then, Amy started to cry. Her block tower kept falling over. As Valerie reached out to comfort her, the doorbell rang. She hastily unplugged the iron, not wanting to leave it where Amy could reach it, and carried it with her to open the door. Amy crawled over and pulled on her pant leg.

"Hi, there," her sister Sue laughed as she surveyed the scene. "I see you have your hands full!" She plunked three-year-old Matthew down. Amy was immediately occupied with her older cousin. Valerie abandoned the iron in the kitchen and hung up the shirts she hadn't gotten to yet. She was secretly glad that Sue was early. Now she could put off ironing.

Within a few minutes, two other neighbors had arrived and the children were busy playing. Nancy filled everyone in on her new job, a typing position two days a week at a doctor's office. Valerie looked after Nancy's daughter on those days, but she secretly wished their positions could be reversed. She would love to earn some money and feel like she was using her intelligence once in a while.

When they all left at 2:00, Valerie let out a long sigh. Could she sneak in a nap with Amy? Or should she tidy up? She voted for tidying. It was likely that the house would be a disaster area in a few hours if she didn't do some preemptive work. All the neighborhood children liked to congregate at her house to play. Valerie felt like the neighborhood mother hen, but she loved it.

Yet she knew things were changing. Nine-year-old Judy still had her friends over, but her son, Kevin, had withdrawn, often choosing to sit in his room and read. There was nothing wrong with reading, she kept telling herself, and he read better than most other sixth graders. But she wished that Kevin still wanted to socialize a bit more. Maybe if Bill would teach him golf or spend more time with him. But Bill took little initiative with their son. Her husband had never been a go-getter, although he was stable, loyal, and honest. She respected and loved him. She just wished . . . No, she wouldn't let herself think that way. She would ask the ladies at the Bible study tomorrow morning what they thought about Kevin's shyness. A lot of them had sons. Maybe this was normal?

With her daughter Judy it was the opposite problem. Judy always had plenty of friends, but lately it seemed that her friends mattered more to Judy than Valerie did. And these were new friends, not the same ones Judy had had since she was tiny. Valerie wasn't sure what she thought of them. They were at her house many days, but she could never seem to really talk to them. Tonight, Valerie decided, she and Judy would have a talk. She wanted to make sure that Judy understood how much she loved her and wanted to see her grow into a beautiful woman.

As Valerie finished the ironing, she heard her older two arrive home. She called out to greet them, but as she reached the vestibule, the only evidence of Kevin was his school bag, coat, and shoes, all lying in the middle of the hallway where he had dropped them. Valerie summoned him back. He arrived, sulking, picked up everything, then retreated back upstairs. Judy breathlessly asked if Rachel could stay, and Valerie agreed. Soon other girls arrived to join them, and they took over the living room.

Valerie turned her attention toward dinner. What could she make that would put Bill in a better mood? She really loved him, and he was so much fun when he wanted to be. But lately he'd been brooding. She was frustrated with him, but knew her frustration would only make things worse between them. She put her energy into fried chicken instead.

As she began to set the table, the doorbell rang. It was Mrs. Price, her older next-door neighbor, come to return a book. At least that was the pretense, but Valerie knew she just wanted to chat.

When Bill arrived home a few minutes later, Mrs. Price left, promising to come back at seven. The other girls also made a quick retreat home, though their absence, too, would only be temporary. The whole neighborhood would be there at seven to watch television. They were the first family on their block to get a television, and everyone now congregated in her living room on Tuesday nights. Valerie felt some ambivalence about the TV. It was great fun watching it, and she loved playing hostess. But since they'd bought both it and the new washer, Bill had been more worried about money.

After dinner, she asked Judy to quickly clean the bathroom, while Kevin helped dry the dishes. He whined, but did them anyway. It was their ritual, spending time together each night, and Valerie felt that Kevin relied on it, too.

When the neighbors arrived at seven, Valerie was handed a coffee-cake, two containers of cupcakes, and mountains of banana bread, Mrs. Price's specialty. Judy helped her put them on platters, and then quickly ran off to her room with two giggling neighborhood girls. They wouldn't watch television. They had some things to talk about. Valerie wished she could still be privy to these conversations but sighed, knowing that was impossible, and decided to enjoy her neighbors. She glanced at her husband, who was reliving Sunday's football game with three men. She smiled, happy to see him happy. She hoped it would last.

Carissa, 2014

"Blast!" Carissa had a few other choice words she would have liked to use, but such things rarely came out of her mouth. She looked at Sarah, her two-year-old, with affection, and scooped her up. "What am I going to do with you today? I wasn't expecting this!" She glanced around the living room and sighed. Toys were strewn everywhere. She knew that it was just as bad upstairs. And the laundry hamper was overflowing. She had planned to catch up on housework today, but her plans had just been changed by a phone call.

When Carissa had accepted the casual nursing position at the hospital, she'd been elated. Seven shifts a month—fewer than two a week—and lots of time for her family. She hadn't thought she would be able to find another nursing position so easily when they'd moved to Chicago six months ago. But she had, and it seemed the ideal job. Until today. She had been warned that she might be called in unex-pectedly, and today was one of those times. She had an hour and a half to clean up the house, arrange for someone to look after Sarah, and get to work. And she hadn't even showered yet!

"Better get moving—right, sweetie?" She grabbed the hamper to throw in a load of laundry while she dialed the phone, trying to find a babysitter. Her regular sitter wasn't free Mondays. Then she noticed the bedroom floor. Rick had left yesterday's clothes piled in the corner. She grabbed them with a touch of resentment and headed down the stairs, dialing as she went.

An hour later she was in the car, rushing to her job at the hospital, after frantically dropping Sarah off at Jill's. Jill, a friend from church, had three children under four and didn't like to babysit as a rule, but in a pinch she was willing to help out. Carissa was grateful for her. When Rick had been transferred here from Kansas six months ago, Carissa had left behind her mother, who had been her most reliable babysitter. The kids loved Grandma, and they missed her.

She's not all they miss, thought Carissa wistfully. Her son Gregory had completely changed since moving here. He was twelve and had always been a very outgoing boy, playing Little League, and participating in Kids' Club night at their church. But now he was popular in a whole new way. He had started dressing in black and spending time at the homes of two friends whom Carissa hardly knew. She tried to have the kids over to her house as much as possible, but when they came, they huddled in Greg's room with the door shut, playing video games. In fact, that's pretty much all Greg did now. To make matters worse, the games were multiplayer, which meant that Greg was playing against strangers from all over the country. Carissa wanted to take the game console away, but she was afraid that Greg would completely rebel, and she didn't know how she could handle that.

Rick dealt with the video game obsession by yelling at Greg that he was lazy, which alienated him further. And Rick was home so much less than he had been in Kansas, when he had just been a bank manager. Now he was vice president of corporate affairs, and his hours were so much longer. Quite often he wasn't even home for days at a time, since he traveled a lot. It made Carissa feel guilty for working.

Michelle hadn't fared much better. The teachers in Kansas had often said she was very bright but had a hard time concentrating. The teachers here said she was unmanageable without medication. The doctors agreed that she had ADD, and Carissa had reluctantly started Michelle on Ritalin. She had to admit Michelle was better behaved, though she was still a handful. She had enrolled her in ballet and gymnastics, hoping that physical outlets and planned activities would help her.

"Ballet! Oh, no!" Carissa let her forehead rest for a moment on the steering wheel as she sat at the red light. She had arranged for Michelle to go to Jill's house after school, but had totally forgotten about her ballet lesson. Michelle would just have to miss it. She couldn't ask Jill to drive her—not with those three little kids of her own plus Sarah to manage today. Carissa felt guilty again, causing Michelle to miss something she liked just so Carissa could go to work.

Ballet wasn't the only thing that was going to be missed today. She and Rick had a meeting with Greg's teacher and principal. Greg had taken an aptitude test and had scored in the top 2 percent, which had thrilled Rick to no end. But his teachers were concerned because Greg wasn't applying himself. They wanted to meet with Carissa and Rick to talk about how to help Greg. But Rick said he couldn't skip out in the middle of the day, so it was left to Carissa. And now Carissa wouldn't make it either. The principal had been sympathetic when she called and had rescheduled for the next day. But Carissa wished she could find some way to put her family first.

Her day was long, but her nursing duties took her mind off her worries. She checked in with Jill at four. Her friend sounded frazzled, but said everybody was behaving. Michelle was even helping with the little ones. Gregory didn't answer the phone. He was on the Internet again. She had tried to convince Rick to install parental controls on his computer, but Greg wouldn't stand for it, and Rick couldn't figure his way around the computer Greg had built. Secretly Carissa wondered if that was just an excuse, since a few times lately when she walked in on Rick on the computer he had minimized the screen awfully quickly. What if Gregory weren't the only one with the problem? Carissa didn't think she had the energy to deal with that.

She and Rick just hadn't connected in the same way since moving. She only had a vague idea of what he even did at work. And at the office, Rick had three assistants—very pretty, young assistants—waiting on him hand and foot. Carissa looked down at her own spreading waistline and grimaced. Sometimes she wondered if Rick was lying to her when he said he found her attractive. All the women at work were bright, ambitious, beautiful, and childless. She couldn't measure up.

As she drove home, she passed through the neighborhood where her church's small group study met. She loved Thursday nights. It was the one time during the week when she felt like she actually belonged in Chicago. It had been so hard to make friends since moving here, and she and Rick were always so busy. She was still a half hour away from home, the house Rick had insisted on buying in a prestigious neighborhood.

At first she had loved the house, sharing Rick's excitement. But that new thrill had quickly evaporated. No one on the street was ever home during the day, so Carissa had no one to talk to. And the house was so huge that it was just too much to clean! She pulled into the driveway, Sarah asleep in the car seat, and Michelle talking a mile a minute, complaining about missing ballet. When Carissa opened the door, she was greeted by the disaster in the living room she'd left that morning. She knew she should ask Michelle to clean up her own things, but Michelle was already angry with her.

Instead, Carissa let the kids scatter on computers and iPads while she prepared dinner. Once everything was in the oven, she started tidying. She wondered if Rick would make it home to eat. And glancing down the hall to Gregory's room, she wondered if her son would want to join them.

What's Wrong with Me?

When we think about our jobs as mothers and wives, we often think women in centuries past performed these roles much better than we do. We ask ourselves, "What's wrong with me? Why can't I cope? Why am I always so tired?" What I hope I've shown through these three stories is that these are the wrong questions to be asking. Instead of blaming ourselves for how out of control we feel, we should realize that feeling out of control is the logical outcome of our busy society. There's nothing necessarily wrong with us; there may be something wrong with how busy our lives are.

Even though these stories were fictional, they're typical of how people lived at different periods in our history. In each time period, women were essentially concerned with the same things: how to raise their children to love God; how to have an intimate marriage; how to promote sibling harmony; and how to provide financial stability to their families.

These are the questions that should still occupy our attention, since they crystallize our priorities. And when we focus on these questions, we can stop giving ourselves such a hard time and start coming up with practical solutions!

The answers to these questions, though, were often easier to find in the past. Let's look at the different ways this was true.

Community

Perhaps the biggest change over the years is the disappearance of a strong, binding community. Meg, in the 1860s, lived right next door to the children's grandparents, aunts, uncles, and cousins, all of whom could offer advice and encouragement. The pastor was an important person in the town, and neighbors were often quick to help discipline when necessary. They did not worry about their children being out alone; they knew somebody would look out for them.

Valerie's family of the 1950s was important to her, too. Her sister socialized with her and offered advice, and she had friends on her street to talk to. Though the town was not as cohesive as Meg's, Valerie lived in a real neighborhood. She had lived in her house for years and likely would stay in the same house for many years to come.

Carissa's life in the world today is very different. Her husband's job has taken them across the country and away from her support system. She doesn't know very many people in town and has had a hard time meeting friends. She is worried about negative influences on her son, but she has little support in dealing with his problems. In fact, the people of her church are her only source of support. But even in an emergency, she feels guilty having to find a new babysitter from among them. Instead of having people to rely on, Carissa lives in an age and place where everyone has to fend for himself or herself.

The Importance of the Family

In the 1800s, women were excluded from voters' lists, public office, university posts, church office, legal economic protection, and much else. For the most part, a woman's world revolved around her family's economic and social relationships.[1] Everything she did concerned the home. Even though each member of the family had defined tasks, and the husband was the home's authority figure, the family was a working partnership. In our story, Meg was involved in her husband Paul's job. She knew the intricacies of the farm, and she contributed to its success.

Over the next century, women made incredible legal and economic gains. Yet a more insidious change took place. As the family's economic core left the home to move to a factory or an office, the wife was suddenly excluded from the economic survival of the family. Men became superfluous to the home, and women to the world of work. Valerie bemoans the fact that she's left alone while her husband has more intellectual challenges, and Carissa and Rick seem almost to inhabit two different worlds. While we may rightly applaud the rights women won in the twentieth century, we often forget what was lost: the family working together.

The Role of Outside Work

While at one time work and home couldn't be separated, by the early part of this century they were quite distinct. Men began searching for work away from the farm, for the simple reason that, for most, the farm was no longer a stable source of income. There's no doubt that probably the best benefit families have found over the last century is that most no longer live at the edge of poverty.

In 1900, 56 percent of American families lived at the edge of poverty,[2] compared to just 15 percent today.[3] Nevertheless, in this quest to become more affluent, husbands left home in unprecedented numbers. The father thus becomes a distant figure in the family, defined mostly by his status as a breadwinner. Where he was once very much involved in the family's life, as Paul was in disciplining Jacob, today he may not even make it home for dinner.

Women don't escape this identity trap either. The jobs women have traditionally done, like housework and child care, earn no money, so they're devalued. All of us are judged on an economic basis, something that would never have happened when the house was the place of business.

The Role of Women

By the middle of the twentieth century, women were defined by how well they could keep a comfortable home and raise good children. It's interesting that the woman described in Proverbs 31, often considered the biblical epitome of womanhood, probably best describes our 1860s woman, Meg. She was active in every sphere of life.

The Role of Children

Almost as profound as the change in the role of women is that of the role of children. They were once economically vital to the family. Even the fact that we have summer holidays from school hearkens back to the days when children were needed to work on the farm during the summer.

Up until very recently, children were still expected to contribute to the family: they went to school but also had to do chores. Today, though, psychologists warn us we have to do everything right or we'll mess our children up for life. Combine that attitude with society's rampant consumerism, and we have awfully pampered children. We enroll them in after-school activities to give them every opportunity. We buy them tons of toys. Yet when they don't serve an integral productive role in society, it's easy for them to become negative and self-absorbed.

Our culture today seems to work against positive parenting. In the 1950s, the television set was actually a community builder. Today, 56 percent of children aged eight to sixteen have their own television sets in their rooms. The family has become more splintered than ever.[4] And the computer plays havoc with our children in ways that we can only guess.

Where Does This Leave Us?

When we think of recapturing the "good ol' days," we usually mean returning to the 1950s when life seemed so much more cut-and-dried. Yet a better picture of healthy interdependent relationships might be Meg and Paul, who both played important roles in all aspects of the economic and family life.

Obviously we can't return to the 1800s, and we likely wouldn't want to. I like my iPad too much. But it is useful to look at how life has changed. One of the reasons you're feeling stressed today is because things are more difficult than they were when our mothers were young! It's not that your mother and grandmother did a better job than you do; it's that they did a *different* job. Women in earlier generations weren't perfect; they just had different things to cope with, and had more community resources to help them along the way. When we realize this, we can stop blaming ourselves for being so lazy and start looking for some practical solutions that can help us find some of that community and purpose that Meg had.

Quick Reality Check

What pressures in parenting and work do you face that are new in our culture? Have you ever thought of them this way? Do you think you can forgive yourself for not being perfect, knowing that you are charting new territory?

For Deeper Thought

Do you compare yourself to your mother or your grandmother? Do you feel you have to do as good a job as older women did when they had younger families? Remember that God has given you a specific task to be done today—not in 1850 or even 1950.

Chapter 3

This Ain't My Mama's House!

*D*uring a sociology seminar on technology, my university professor asked the class to choose our favorite of three Star Trek gadgets: the holodeck, the transporter, or the replicator. For those of you who are not "Trekkies," the holodeck is the ultimate virtual reality machine, which allows you to step into a room and experience any fantasy world you want; the transporter sends you anywhere you want to go immediately; and the replicator creates any food you want instantly. Everyone chose one of the first two gadgets. I was the only one who chose the replicator, the ultimate time-saver in a busy home. I guess I've always been a realist, but it seemed to me that saving time at day-to-day tasks was infinitely better than a nice vacation.

You probably don't need a study to tell you that housework can bring your mood plummeting. You usually do it alone, nobody thanks you when you finish something, and besides that, it's never really done! Anyone who has ever tried to sweep a floor only to notice that your toddler is trailing you eating a box of crackers knows that household chores can take their toll. So it's no wonder that studies have verified that housework can be one of the most depressing jobs, whether you're doing a whole day of it or just fifteen minutes of dishes.

> *Face it . . . housework's depressing!*

Society's Housework Standards

Nevertheless, one of the ironies of housework is that an alien visiting our planet would think that it was the most rewarding activity on earth. In commercials for household cleaners, women look as if they have found their purpose in life by making their homes sparkle. All of this advertising is designed to make us think we must have homes like that to be happy. If we don't, we should be ashamed of ourselves; that level of cleanliness is always attainable with enough effort and the right products.

Did you know that one hundred years ago no one used deodorant? Some company discovered how to make it, but then they had to find a way to market it. They ran magazine ads informing people that everyone stank. Until then, body odor hadn't been much of an issue—everyone smelled the same. All of a sudden, it became a social disgrace, and today almost everyone uses deodorant.

The same methods have been used for household cleaning products. Very few of these products were in existence one hundred years ago. People didn't have the time or the ability to get things that clean. Meg, in our story, only had four small rooms to clean, and little furniture to dust. Yet despite all the new products, we are spending more time on housework today than people did one hundred years ago. Why?

Because standards are completely different. During the 1920s, when society was booming, many new cleaning products were introduced, and it soon became a status symbol to have a very clean house. The status symbol for women during World War II was helping with the war effort. But as soon as the war ended, women were pressured to leave the workforce and raise families. The status symbol became not just a clean house but a clean house with a wife at home who did everything, just like Valerie in our story.

But it hasn't stopped there. In the last generation, blenders, food processors, and bread and pasta makers have become standard fare in many kitchens. Though gadgets may save time at individual tasks, the cumulative effect of them has simply been to increase what is expected of us. Washing machines mean we wash clothes more often so we do more laundry. Bread and pasta makers mean we make things from scratch that we once may have bought. Because all these gadgets make perfect cleanliness and gourmet meals possible, we're now held to a far higher standard than women were generations ago.

Myth #1: The Perfect Housewife

It's hardly surprising that women have internalized all these perfection messages. We expect ourselves to live up to some ideal. The most enduring is what I call the myth of the perfect housewife. Here, the only way for a woman to prove herself is by excelling at her housework role. Work outside the home is frowned upon, or at least seen as secondary in importance, and a woman is judged by whether or not her house is clean. Though far more common a generation ago than it is today, many of its expectations are still with us. So it's hardly surprising that housework has the moral connotations for women that it does.

Even for those of us who don't strive for "immaculate," this societal standard still affects us. Living in a messy house is often a source of tension for us in a way that it rarely is for men. Women tend to be nesters, wanting to create a comfortable physical family environment. It is expected of us, and we in turn expect it of ourselves.

I have never been a super cleaner; I always seem to have so many projects on the go that my house is hard to keep clutter-free. Some of my friends, though, seem to live straight out of *Better Homes and Gardens* (except on a budget!). I go into their homes and can't help but compare them to my own cluttered house. I feel a sense of shame in a way that I don't if I'm in the presence of a woman with perfectly manicured hands (something else I haven't mastered) or even a high-powered career. Somehow my house, too often, becomes a measuring stick in a way few other things do.

Keeping a clean, comfortable home can be a true service to our families. But if we allow it to be a source of tension and stress, we need to seriously reexamine our motives. Have we accepted what society tells us a woman's job is? Or will we make those decisions ourselves based on a truer standard?

Myth #2: Superwoman

The next myth is a more modern one, demanding that women excel at everything, including a career. So we spin so hard trying to make sure we look like we have everything under control that we don't take a step back and ask if we really even want all of these roles.

Maybe we work outside the home harder than we need to because that's what people expect of us. A woman completing her pediatric residency with my husband, Keith, called me for advice on her maternity leave. Her sixteen weeks were almost over, and she was required to go back to work. But if she juggled vacations and light rotations, she could get an extra eight weeks with her baby. She was worried about what her supervisors would think about her dedication to the job if she took this option. I asked her, "In ten years, what will matter most to you? What your former supervisors thought of you, or how your daughter feels about you?" She quickly made the decision to extend her maternity leave.

Maybe you feel that career and educational demands are eating into your family's needs. Or maybe you simply yearn for more quality time with your children. When my kids were toddlers, I was with them 24/7, every day. Yet that didn't mean that I spent any real time with them. Often my main focus was in keeping them out of my hair so I could get some cleaning done. Work had still taken over my agenda, and the kids had gotten the short end of the stick.

Balance is an awfully tricky thing, and I'm not sure it's ever really attainable. Balance means that you're always going to be saying "no" to something—whether it's your husband or your kids or your job. And none of us likes saying no. Aiming for a truly balanced life, then, just means deciding who you're going to let down. And that's depressing in a whole other way. Maybe instead of having it all it's better to focus on the few things that we feel really called to.

Myth #3: The Reincarnated Mother

Somewhere in between these two is the most dangerous expectation of all: the one that says you must measure up to another individual, often the infamous mother-in-law. If your husband had a mother who did everything for him as a child, he may expect you to do everything, too. And not just do everything, but do it the same way his mother did. Of course this is impossible since you are not his mother. If you're caught up in this dynamic, your relationship with your husband and even your extended family is too easily jeopardized. You resent them for expecting something from you that you can't deliver, and they resent you for not fulfilling your role.

My friend Linda battles this all the time. She is a wonderful wife and mother with a part-time career of her own, and whenever I enter her house I feel like I live in a pigsty compared to her. Yet her husband's mother was so proficient at housework and at dedicating herself to her four children—often to her own detriment—that there is no way Linda can ever re-create that situation. She doesn't cook roasts the same way. She doesn't make the bed the same way. She's constantly exhausted.

For others, the problem is not that your husband expects you to live up to his idea of his mother. Rather, it's that you expect yourself to become your mother. She may not be helping matters, always making suggestions about how you could clean better, or decorate better, or raise your children better. You feel like you will never be good enough.

Finally, there are those of us who are busy raising stepchildren, battling the standard of another woman who cares for the children on alternate weeks. If you feel yourself pressured to fit into someone else's mold, remember that, as Psalm 139 tells us, God made you unique and for a specific purpose. He did not make you an extension of someone else; He simply made you. Pray about what God's purposes are for you, your husband, and your children, and concentrate on these priorities rather than on trying to become someone you were not put on this earth to be.

What Are Your Standards?

We've looked at the roles women often assume in order to live up to some societal ideal, but these aren't the only ways in which we set standards for ourselves. How often do you think you should vacuum? How many times do you wear a pair of pants before you wash them? How often do you change your sheets? We all have varying standards for how frequently we do tasks like these.

It's often hard to admit that the way we do these things is simply that: the way we do things. It is not prescribed by God, the church, our friends, our parents, or anybody other than ourselves. We are the ones who ultimately set the housework standards for our own home. So, if you are aiming for immaculate, and frustrating yourself in the process, reevaluate. See if you can find yourself in one of these categories:

Unattainable standards. Do you have high standards but never achieve them? I fall into this category. I walk through the house thinking, "That floor needs mopping. That carpet needs vacuuming. When will I ever have the time?" Even if you aren't motivated enough to actually clean, you can never fully enjoy what you are doing because you have left housework undone.

Exhausting standards. Are you so preoccupied with achieving your standards that you have no time for anything else? Instead of going outside with your family, you stay inside to clean up after them. Instead of relaxing once children are in bed, you spend the time tidying. The never-ending job takes all of your energy.

Stifling standards. Have you created a home where your family feels stifled? Do you grow agitated if anything gets out of place? Maybe you have confused creating a comfortable home with creating an immaculate home.

Conflicting standards. Do you expect your husband to be as preoccupied with housework as you are? Men are not usually raised to be concerned with housework; women are. It is only natural that they put less of an emphasis on it. If you are waiting for your husband and children to "see the light," you are probably wasting a lot of energy.

Changing Our Housework Patterns

Whether we're trying to live up to some unattainable role, or trying to impose some housework standard on our family, there's no doubt we're hurting ourselves and our relationships in the process. You just can't live like this peaceably forever! So why do we set these standards in the first place? Our standards are so much a part of who we are, bred in us by our families, our friends, the media, and other sources, that we hardly ever question them. If things aren't working, the answer isn't to reevaluate; it's just to work harder!

We need to take a huge step back and look at our lives through God's eyes. The best way to make real change is not to devise elaborate plans or make new resolutions to become the perfect wife and mother. It's to come humbly before God and ask what He thinks is important. Forget your upbringing, your social circle, and even your church for a minute and let's see what God says.

Our starting point should be the verse, "There is now no condemnation for those who are in Christ Jesus" (Rom. 8:1). I know this refers specifically to forgiveness of sins, but there's a principle in there we shouldn't forget. What are the words we associate with our pre-Christian state? I think of law, bondage, slave, and guilt. And the words of our Christian life? Grace, freedom, and forgiveness. Yet do we really experience this freedom? Or as women are we trying to impose a new law upon ourselves, one that crushes us in constant guilt because we can't measure up? Let's stop measuring against society's standard and ask God what He wants us to aim for. Once we know what He wants, we can head in the right direction.

When it comes to our families, I believe there are three questions that God asks us which seem to cover all the bases.

1. Are all your family members looking more like Christ?

First and foremost, God's desire is for us to be "conformed to the likeness of his Son" (Rom. 8:29). Everything we do should contribute to our becoming more like Christ. Like C. S. Lewis once wrote, "Every Christian is to become a little Christ. The whole purpose of becoming a Christian is simply nothing else."[1]

As we do so, we demonstrate the fruits of the Spirit more and more.

Family relationships are vital to learning about God and growing closer to Him. God is by nature relational. He Himself is comprised of three persons, all in relationship with each another. He describes Himself as our Father, our bridegroom, a mother hen, a jealous husband, all roles in a relationship. Children learn about God as a parent through us as parents. And God uses marriage to illustrate His relationship with the church (see Eph. 5:25–33). It is often within relationship that growth toward Christlikeness occurs. So when you're looking at your family patterns, ask yourself if what you are doing is helping your family become more Christlike or not.

2. Are you a good steward of My gifts?

Moving closer to God is the first step to any positive change, but it must be done in conjunction with moving outward to other people. In the parable of the talents, in Matthew 25:14–30, the master, representing God, gave his servants money he wanted them to invest to further his interests. He rewarded those who stepped out and used the money to gain more, but was angered at the servant who hid what he had been given. God wants us to use what He has given us, whether it is one talent or ten, to grow His kingdom.

Let me give you an example. Have you ever been getting out of church when you see a couple whom you just know you'd connect with? You want more friends, and you desperately need some adult conversation, and your husband could use some, too. So you think to yourself, "I'll invite them over for lunch!" You make your way over to the wife, and are about to open your mouth, when you realize your breakfast dishes are still in the sink. There goes that plan. So you say, "I'll call you!" and she agrees. But you never do, because your house is never clean enough. The standards we set for our household can actually discourage us from entertaining others or from letting children play. That puts our focus not on relationships but on our possessions.

And the gifts God gives you aren't all of the material kind. Maybe God made you a wonderful teacher, but you're not leading a Bible study or teaching Sunday school because you're just too busy with other things. Obviously, there are times when we are legitimately unable to serve; but if it's a perpetual problem, then we need to rethink our priorities. Being good stewards of everything God has given you means prioritizing "building up treasures in heaven" rather than protecting treasures here.

3. Are you providing a stumbling block to others?

Finally, there is little that angered Jesus more than people who provided a stumbling block to children. In Luke 17:2, He said, "It would be better for him to be thrown into the sea with a millstone tied around his neck than for him to cause one of these little ones to sin." I don't know about you, but I'd rather steer clear of that millstone thing. Paul, in his first letter to the Corinthians, says that we should also be vitally concerned with the spiritual condition of new Christians (8:9). We should never do anything that hinders anyone's spiritual journey toward Christlikeness.

The problem is that stumbling blocks are awfully easy to put up. Look at your children for a moment. What most benefits them? Scripturally, it's learning how to obey. If the way that you interact with your children prevents them from respecting you, then you are providing a stumbling block that may keep them from learning about God.

Yet it's not just children we can harm. Bill Hybels, senior pastor of Willow Creek Community Church, says that when people today consider their faith, they're not interested in profound arguments. They have a simple question: "Will I be trading up or trading down by becoming a Christian?" If you're unhappy with your role in your family, you're likely telling your non-Christian friends, as well as your kids, that God asks something of you that makes you miserable. To become a Christian, then, may well seem to be trading down for them. Who's going to want to do that?

The solution, of course, is not to put on a happy face and pretend that everything's great. That's a surefire recipe for disaster! It's to go to God and ask Him to clarify what you should be doing. When we're in the midst of God's plan for us, we feel peace. If we don't feel peace where we are, we need to move.

Notice that these three questions seem to have little to do with housework itself and everything to do with furthering God's kingdom. So how do you use these questions to help you practically in deciding your day-to-day activities? I believe that if we have vision, the rest falls into place. Because of this, I'm not going to focus on housework rules themselves, since these vary with each family situation anyway.

Instead, let's focus on how we can reduce our time doing housework. That will give us more time to devote to other worthy pursuits.

While it may sound like housework is unimportant to me, nothing could be further from the truth. It is important to have a comfortable home for your family, to provide a retreat from the world. After all, no one wants to fear catching a communicable disease in your bathroom. There is a certain level of cleanliness that's non-negotiable!

And when your children feel comfortable at home, it is more likely they will invite their friends over to your house, and then you can keep a better eye on them. Neighbors will enjoy visiting, and people will gravitate to you. My concern is that we define cleanliness as comfort, and so neglect the priorities of spiritual growth and good stewardship. We need to find ways to get the housework done as quickly as we can and with as little stress as possible. I have three main strategies to do this: get organized; create low maintenance, family-friendly homes; and schedule other priorities (the third will be covered in the next chapter).

Get Organized!

The most obvious way to cut down on housework time is to do it faster. But the only way you can do this is to get organized. Even if you feel like you're already running full tilt all day, there may be ways you can save time.

Plan

The best example of this is meal planning and preparation. When you don't plan what you're going to make for dinner, you may end up with too much to do—including running to the grocery store—at the last minute. Do some things ahead of time to save yourself the stress. Try to plan your meals for a whole week. If you like, you can gather your family together and let them each choose one meal. This increases the chance they'll eat it, too!

If you're really ambitious, you can try some of the cooking strategies that are available now, such as Mimi Wilson and Mary Beth Lagerborg's *Once-a-Month Cooking*.[2] They advocate setting aside two days in a month to shop, prepare, and freeze all your meals for that month. Preparing beforehand and cooking in bulk can save you time, and best of all can eliminate the frustration you feel when it's dinnertime and you don't have a clue what to make.

Do Two Things at Once

In her book *The Family Manager*, Kathy Peel gives some useful ideas for saving time while doing housework.[3] She advocates doing two things at once as often as you can. Do you have a portable phone? You can clean while you're on hold. Are your children playing in the bath? Take that opportunity to clean out your medicine cabinet.

Maintain

Another thing we can do to reduce the amount of work we do is preventative maintenance. Make a list of all the things in your house that need to be maintained. Here are some of the common ones to get you started:

- Get your furnace and air conditioner serviced yearly.
- Change the filters on furnaces, range hoods, air purifiers, humidifiers, or other appliances.
- Clean out your eaves troughs every year.
- Use a dehumidifier if your basement is damp, and a humidifier if your winters are dry.
- Get carpets cleaned yearly.
- Get furniture cleaned yearly.
- Clean draperies several times a year.
- Move all the furniture and vacuum at least twice a year.
- Strip floors and apply finish at least twice a year.

If you keep up with these chores, you are likely to avoid costly bills, power outages, floods, or mold. And your things will last longer. That will save you time in itself!

Schedule Chores

Schedule time for maintenance, but also consider scheduling time for regular housework tasks. One of the problems people frequently have with housework is that they concentrate on the "visible" areas, like the living room and kitchen, while other areas rarely get cleaned. Or they mop the kitchen floor frequently, but forget to vacuum the upstairs carpets.

That's not a good plan for a comfortable home, because it means parts of your house are bound to get out of control, likely sending you around the bend. If you only dust your bedroom every few months, even though you dust your living room twice weekly (where your guests are!), you may start sneezing all night.

Make a list of how often you want tasks to be done. Ideally, you can ask your family to help with some of them. We'll talk about this later. But for those tasks you've allocated to yourself, decide which need to be done daily, weekly, every other week, and monthly. Make a monthly schedule so you can check off the things as you do them. I've included the one we use to give you a start, as well as a blank one you can adapt for your own needs (see pp. 64–65). Use this schedule to decide how often you want to do your own chores, and then organize yourself to do them.

You'll find several advantages to this system. First, everything that needs to get done will get done. Your house will be well maintained, so your things will last longer. Second, you may actually end up doing less work.

Once you've done your tasks for today, you can stop, even if the laundry room is a mess or papers are threatening to engulf your desk. These things will get taken care of in their own time, and now it's time for you to rest! Similarly, if you do housework according to a schedule, you know that everything will get done in its time. Therefore, once you've finished today's tasks, there's nothing else to do. You can stop without feeling guilty about relaxing or spending time on something else.

Of course, for some of you the opposite will happen. You'll end up doing more work than you had done before, because you honestly didn't clean often enough to keep a consistently clean house. (This is often the case for me, I'll admit.) Let me assure you that, even so, you can learn to do things faster. Here are some suggestions:

- Clean to upbeat, fast music.
- Time yourself and see if you can beat your previous time.
- Think about cleaning as exercise. Even put on workout clothes and your running shoes! Try to clean so fast that you literally work up a sweat and get out of breath. That way, cleaning will count for one of the twenty-minute periods of exercise you're supposed to get each day.

Give Yourself Specific Goals

Has this ever happened to you? You decide to clean your bedroom and in the process find several things that actually belong in the living room. You gather them up and trudge downstairs and notice your plants need watering. When you go to the kitchen to return the watering can, you notice the breakfast dishes are still in the sink. You do those, and then realize you're late picking up your kids from school. You rush out, frustrated because nothing is actually clean.

I do this all the time. It's like I have no attention span when it comes to tidying up. After spending an hour, I'll have a small portion of every room in the house clean, but nothing's actually finished. It feels like I have nothing to show for everything I've done!

When you give yourself a task, make sure you do it and only it. If there's stuff that needs to be moved to another room, make a pile but don't carry it there until you've finished the task at hand. That way you know that at least one room, at the end of all your efforts, is tidy.

Define "Good Enough"

When you clean your living room, do you vacuum under the couches each time? Do you get up on a chair and dust off the top of the bookcase? Do you wash down your venetian blinds? We all have different answers to these questions, and there isn't one right answer. But it's good to think about what, in your mind, constitutes "good enough" when it comes to cleaning a room. You may not always have time for a thorough cleaning, so what can you skip and what's really necessary? If you always demand perfection from yourself, the idea of cleaning may be so overwhelming you can't even start.

Chore to be done	Week 1						Week 2						Week 3						Week 4					
	M	T	W	T	F	S	M	T	W	T	F	S	M	T	W	T	F	S	M	T	W	T	F	S
DAILY																								
Wash dishes																								
Kitchen garbage																								
Wash laundry																								
Fold laundry																								
Sweep floors																								
Make dinner																								
Tidy downstairs																								
Tidy upstairs																								
Prepare next day's lunches																								
WEEKLY																								
Tidy basement / family room																								
Clean bathrooms																								
Take out garbage																								
Dust downstairs																								
Dust upstairs																								
Vacuum carpets																								
Pay bills																								
Do grocery shopping																								
MONTHLY																								
Clean laundry room																								
Mop upstairs																								
Wash windows																								
Reconcile bank statements																								
Clean/change furnace filters																								

Chore to be done	Week 1					Week 2						Week 3						Week 4				
	M	T	W	T	F	S	M	T	W	T	F	S	M	T	W	T	F	S	M	T	W	T	F	S
DAILY																								
WEEKLY																								
MONTHLY																								

What is good enough? If you don't have time to do everything you'd like to do every week, maybe you can do some of those things once a month, or once a season, and just do the necessities every week. Decide what's adequate, and don't berate yourself for not meeting a higher standard.

Create a Family-Friendly Home

If you buy beautiful furniture and gorgeous carpets, chances are you'll be preoccupied with cleanliness. Have you ever been in a house where you were afraid you might stain the coffee table or inadvertently break some crystal? Does your house make you nervous? If it does, it probably worries others, too. Don't use your home to measure your material success; use it to nurture your family.

If you have children at home, consider buying gently used furniture at auctions, garage sales, and secondhand stores. When you have small children, use plastic dishes, and buy tables and chairs you can wipe down rather than wooden antiques. Buy slipcovers (or make your own) that are easily washable.

During his residency, my husband studied an old case of a mother who suspected her three-year-old son had a behavioral problem. Other caregivers who knew the child well felt he was perfectly normal. When a house visit was conducted it was soon clear what the problem was. The mother was trying to maintain the home as neatly as it had been before he was born. There were no toys anywhere. The magazines were fanned out over the coffee table. In his room, the closets were color-coded alphabetically (blue T-shirts in front of green T-shirts in front of red T-shirts). You can just imagine this woman's stress whenever her little boy tried to act like a child and explore the house. Something might get out of place!

If you find that your standards are too stifling for your family, give them a place where they can exercise their own standards. This may encourage them to respect yours in the rest of the house. If you already have expensive furniture, then try creating at least one room of the house where your children can let loose. For teenagers, make sure that there's a comfy area where they can socialize, spill chips, or put their feet up without provoking your ire. For smaller kids, make sure there's a place they can be creative with paint, Play-Doh, or glue. Children may actually enjoy living in an environment that is messy. For some it's a way to assert their independence. Just because your eleven-year-old son wants to keep his room like a pigsty doesn't mean that he will grow up to be a vagrant. To avoid conflict, try allowing your children to keep their rooms as they would like. In return, you can ask them to clean them (not necessarily tidy, but clean) once a week. That way you know dust isn't building up and dirty laundry is getting cleaned, even if pieces of model airplanes are still scattered around the room.

As you change your emphasis to people's comfort, rather than keeping up appearances, your attitude toward housework will probably change as well. Having the "perfect house" as a standard can be exhausting, constricting our willingness to share with others, because our house is never ready.

When we think this way, we are putting things ahead of people. Creating a family-friendly home means creating a home where people feel comfortable. Our aim is to share our homes and our lives, not to put on a show. So instead of putting your energy into keeping a perfect home that few see, try creating a comfortable one that people feel welcome in.

Working efficiently, organizing well, and making your home family friendly can help free your time and reduce your stress. It can give you more opportunities to focus on your eternal goals rather than running around trying to keep everything perfect. In the next chapter we'll look at a third strategy: refocusing our lives on our eternal goals by scheduling time to meet our true priorities.

Quick Reality Check

Who sets your standards? Can you recognize yourself in any of the myths? Do you try to be a perfect housewife? A superwoman? Are you trying to be someone else, like your mother or mother-in-law? Ask God for a vision of your uniqueness.

———————— *For Deeper Thought* ————————

1. What are your standards like? Do you have unattainable standards, exhausting standards, stifling standards, conflicting standards, or even some combination of these? What would you most like to change?

2. Are there areas where better planning could save you time? Look at the suggestions for better planning and more efficient housework, and ask which would make the most difference to you.

3. How much time would you like to spend on housework? Write down the activities you do and decide how much time ideally you would like to spend at each thing. Make sure that those that matter most to you get a fair amount of time. Now write down how much time you actually spend at these things. Where are the biggest discrepancies?

Chapter 4

Balancing Tipped Scales

*J*f you had been hired to clean your home, you would have a designated start time and a designated finish time, and you would try to be as efficient as possible during that time so you could finish early. The problem with doing your own housework is that you are always at work when you are at home. Even when you're sitting down relaxing, you may stare off into space and, in the process, notice that your walls need cleaning.

The best way to stop yourself from working all the time—or at least feeling like you have to, even if you don't—is to schedule other activities and make them your first priority. These activities should be the really important things that help keep your life focused and you more contented. That way, you are taking responsibility for your own happiness. Even if nothing else changes, you do not have to stay in the same rut.

After all, the reason that we're so exhausted is because we're spending so much of our time on things that exhaust us. Either our lives are consumed with the "work" of child care and running a family, or we're wasting time to deal with that exhaustion. And wasting time always makes you feel more tired, anyway. So if you want to feel less tired, add more of the things that feed your soul, and let them crowd out the things that exhaust you.

New Priorities and Your Family

Not only will this help you feel rejuvenated, it will also help to transform your relationships with your children. Kids feel free to grow and explore when they know that you have more in your life than just them. They will also benefit from your model of balance in their future relationships and gender identities. Your daughters are less likely to completely surrender their own needs for the family's sake. Neither are they as likely to reject the homemaker role completely to pursue only a career, as many women have done to avoid the unfulfilling lives they believe their mothers had.[1] Your sons can then understand that, while motherhood is extremely important, God gave you other talents and goals as well. They will be more likely to treat their own wives with respect and so have stronger marriages.

Maybe you're saying, "But I already work outside the home, so obviously my kids see me as balanced." To a certain extent you may be right. But if they see you desperately trying to get everything done whenever you're not at work, they may think of you as a martyr. And that's hardly a balanced life!

Finally, your relationship with your husband is likely to improve in the long run if he feels that you have interests outside the family. A common complaint from married couples with a stay-at-home mother is that, when the husband gets home from work, he wants half an hour to himself to unwind, while his wife is desperate for adult conversation.

As you develop more outlets for your legitimate needs, you will rely on him less as your only source of adult companionship. You can approach him as an equal who wants to spend time with him and not as someone who is too clingy or needy.

The New Priorities Model

And what are these priorities? Our lives should be filled with (1) a deep spiritual life, (2) strong relationships, and (3) a healthy body and a peaceful mind. Instead, too often they're filled with Facebook, Pinterest, and too much guilt for the stuff we're not getting done. When we start making an effort to fill our lives with things that help us feel more purposeful, more relaxed, and more at peace, we'll find that a lot of that guilt and angst evaporates. Here's a quick look at each area that needs our attention.

1. Spiritual Care
Time in the Word

Nothing compares with reading the Scriptures to saturate us in the truth and remind us of the joy that is found simply in resting in God. Scriptures help put your problems in perspective, give you biblical guidelines for your family, and increase your love and patience. But it can be hard to find the time to read them, especially when you're exhausted. Keep a pocket-sized New Testament handy. You can read while you are nursing your baby, commuting to work, waiting in the car for your child to be finished with lessons, even on an exercise machine.

I once read that when Billy Graham's wife, Ruth, was caring for their young children, she bought a Bible on tape to listen to while she was cleaning her house. For her, finding time to sit down and read was almost impossible. Music can also be used to help us meditate on the Word of God. The lyrics of many praise CDs are primarily from Scripture. Turning on a Christian CD while dusting can lift your spirits and help you to feel the presence of God. Using any creative method you can find, I encourage you to fill your life with Scripture.

Sometimes, though, we need times to just be quiet before God; a time simply to listen to what He has to say. Though most of us would love to hear a voice from the sky, more often He speaks to us in a whisper, like He did to Elijah. To hear that whisper, we need to be still and know that He is God (Ps. 46:10). Being still is awfully hard, but try to snatch a few minutes every day when you can simply listen, perhaps journaling the thoughts He gives you, so that your soul can feel true rest.

While maintaining our personal relationship with God is vital, it's also important that we meet with other Christians. Sunday morning services can be very uplifting, but often they're not enough to sustain us. In most churches Sundays are teaching time; they are not times for relationship building. And it is these relationships that can keep you accountable, help you keep your perspective, and nurture and challenge you.

We moved to a smaller town when my children were preschoolers, and one of the best benefits for me was getting the chance to attend a women's Bible study. For stay-at-home moms, midweek daytime studies can literally be a godsend. Ours provides babysitting, and it's a refreshing break during the week. Of the twenty or so evangelical churches in our town, only five offer midweek daytime studies. Women from all different kinds of churches attend these. If your church doesn't have a women's study, find another church in your area that does!

If a daytime study doesn't work for you, look for a small group that meets in the evenings. Many churches offer studies midweek in people's homes. This can be a wonderful source for encouragement. If babysitting is an issue, consider doing what my friends Barb and Tom do and host one in your house. Or, you can choose the route that Aimee and Paul took and organize a small group that meets at the church itself. There they have access to large play areas for the children, and everybody pools their money to hire one or two sitters for all the children. You can even meet earlier and then share dinner together. It's a perfect chance for community building.

What if you work odd hours and you can't commit to a regular study? Or what if you spend so much time at work you don't want to be away from home another night of the week? Consider starting a study or prayer group at work. Even if you know only one other Christian in your office, chances are, if you start meeting together, other Christians would pop out of the woodwork and join you. Many large cities also have lunch hour meetings in the downtown core. When I was nineteen and working at a summer job in one of the giant skyscrapers of Toronto, I attended an incredibly alive evangelistic lunchtime meeting in the boardroom of a major insurance company. If you work in a downtown area, see if something meets near you.

> **SPIRITUAL CARE IDEAS**
>
> - Read Scripture.
> - Memorize Scripture.
> - Read inspirational books— or listen to them while you commute.
> - Listen to the Bible on tape.
> - Listen to praise CDs.
> - Join a women's Bible study.
> - Join a small group Bible study.
> - Start a small group at school or work.

Take time to nurture your spiritual side, and you will get the food you need to keep the rest of your life in perspective.

Time Serving Others

Often, the best way to help yourself is to help someone else. When we serve others (and I mean those outside of our family), we are drawn outside of our limited scope to see more of God's creation and His purpose. Tony Campolo relates the story of a woman who had been suffering from depression for years and visiting a psychotherapist frequently to discuss her problems. She became involved with Campolo's inner-city missions to children, and through working with these kids found herself transformed. Serving others did her more good than her therapist![2]

There are times in our lives, though, when we might have to abandon traditional Christian service. When I was juggling nursing one child and running after a toddler, I found it impossible to be involved at church. It required going someplace at specific times when I didn't have a babysitter. But there are still things one can do when our lives are just too chaotic for regular volunteer activities. If your children are young, consider these options:

- Invite a lonely person over to dinner. (They don't mind the chaos of a house with small children nearly as much as you assume they will.)
- Lead a Bible study at your house with a friend who is searching.
- Help at the local food bank one Saturday morning a month. (Many are happy to have children come along.)
- Babysit for a single parent.
- Write letters on behalf of Christians imprisoned for their faith around the world. Join Voice of the Martyrs to get information on how to be a part of a letter-writing campaign.
- Write letters to politicians expressing biblical views on current issues.

As your kids get a little older, you'll want to introduce them to the joy in service. Here are some ideas that can include the whole family:

- Provide child care at a self-help group in your community or church.
- Lend your neighbors a hand by raking leaves, mowing the grass, or gardening.
- Host a summer evangelistic day camp in your backyard.
- Adopt an immigrant family. Get connected through the United Way or Salvation Army, and then show them around the city, where to shop, where to go to church, where to find basic services, and help them adjust to the culture.
- Clean up a local park.
- Do fund-raisers for World Vision, Save the Children, or other charities that your children like. Wash cars, save pennies, collect bottles, or anything else your children like to do. Make a difference!

You can probably think of many other ideas. Making service part of your everyday life keeps your eyes off of yourself, and reminds both you and your family of all the blessings that God has given you!

2. Relationship Care

Family Fun

Laughing together creates family memories. And laughter doesn't have to cost money, and it doesn't have to take too much time! Here are some ideas for young children:

- Curl up in your bed with them and read stories.
- Bake cookies.
- Have a water fight.
- Make play dough or finger paint.
- Go out after the rain and jump in puddles with them.
- Go to the library.
- Run through the sprinkler with them.
- Make a huge ice-cream sundae for breakfast (on weekends, of course!).
- Play Twister.
- Have fashion shows with your dress-up clothes.

- Draw faces on your children.
- Let kids put makeup on you!
- Have a picnic.
- Play video games with them. (They'll probably win and like it!)

With teenagers, activities might be harder to find since being with you isn't "cool." But here are some that may work:

- Go bike riding.
- Ask for your daughter's help to update your wardrobe.
- Play their favorite board games, like Scrabble, Monopoly, etc.
- Volunteer together.
- Attend sports/music/drama functions they're involved in.
- Host teenage get-togethers at your house.
- Watch a movie at home together, complete with popcorn.
- Watch some of their favorite silly YouTube videos.
- Send them a "thinking of you" text once a day.
- Have dessert before dinner.

Couple Time

It's easy for your husband to come last since everything else demands your immediate attention: the children, the dishes, the dog. Yet a happy marriage takes time, too. We'll discuss innovative ways to enhance your couple life in the chapter on intimacy later.

Socializing with Friends

Too often women deprive themselves of the joy of friendship because they don't have time. My husband and I moved to Toronto for his residency when I was three months pregnant (and very sick) with our first child. Because I had a miserable pregnancy and he had an equally miserable schedule, we didn't make very many friends before Rebecca was born.

Two other pregnancies and babies quickly followed, and the end result was that after four years of living in the city, we did very little socializing. The turning point for me came when I joined a playgroup and was finally able to relax with other women during the day. Though many of these women may not have been in my natural social circle in other circumstances, the joy of having someone—anyone—to talk to was worth it.

If you're a naturally shy person, making friends may be difficult. Try doing things you really enjoy. Volunteer at your kids' school, take art classes, go jogging, or do whatever else interests you. You will probably find people with similar interests to yours. Joining a playgroup, a women's Bible study, or a small cell group is another way to meet women in similar life situations to yours. Here are some other ideas:

- Join a women's Bible study group.
- Take a continuing education class.
- Join a gym.
- Join a playgroup if you have young children.
- Join the PTA if your children are in school.
- Volunteer anywhere that inspires you—you'll find people with similar interests.
- Start going for walks early in the morning or after dinner. You'll meet neighbors who are out doing the same thing.
- Shop at the same stores. You'll become familiar to more people or maybe meet some kindred spirits.
- Invite your children's friends' families over to dinner. Your children will appreciate you for it, and you may meet some new friends yourself.

Sometimes husbands resent the times we spend with friends instead of with them. For many men, the issue is simply jealousy. There is no easy way around this, but I suggest talking openly with your husband about your need for a variety of people in your life. Then see if you can schedule some special time with your husband as well. Make sure he understands that you are not rejecting him, only trying to widen your own experiences. If, however, your husband is controlling of your time, or cutting you off from your family and friends, his behavior may be abusive. If your husband is treating you in this way, please seek help from a qualified counselor.

3. Personal Care

Physical Exercise

Research consistently proves that exercise, a healthy diet, and sleep help reduce stress, give you more energy, and boost your spirits. I recently began exercising several times a week and eating better, and I feel much more energetic. (I'm even writing this book!) But I know that finding time to exercise—especially when you have small children—is extremely difficult.

If you do have a reliable babysitter, joining a gym can be a lifesaver. It can give you a much-needed opportunity to get out by yourself and meet new friends. Some gyms even have a babysitting option. Many family gyms like the YMCA offer wonderful children's programs, often starting as young as twelve months, so your whole family can become more active.

But if getting out to a gym is impossible for you, try walking places instead of driving. Go biking, skating, or skiing with your children, or any other activity that gets you active. This gives you a perfect opportunity to communicate with your children without the distractions of television and telephones.

Exercise time does not have to be work. You can use exercise time as play time. If your kids are young, try some of these ideas:

- Chase kids around the yard or basement; play tag, freeze, or hide-and-seek.
- Dance and jump to tapes, action-song videos, or even kid-fitness YouTube videos.
- Practice throwing, kicking, and catching a ball.
- Have a clean-up race: set the timer for five minutes and see how much you all can tidy up.
- Act out stories you read. My family likes Maurice Sendak's *Where the Wild Things Are* and Eric Carle's *From Head to Toe*.
- Have tickle fights or play wrestling matches.
- Join play gym groups at the local YMCA or gym. You'll use gym equipment you wouldn't normally have and meet other neighborhood families.

If you have older kids, try some of these ideas:

- Jog to the corner store and reward your kids with a healthy treat.
- Have skipping contests.
- Play hopscotch.
- Find a family sport, like skating, skiing, biking, or basketball; hold sports parties for the neighborhood.
- Take camping holidays, and canoe, hike, and swim.
- Play Frisbee in the park.
- Go tobogganing.

As you become more active with your children, they will probably have more fun with you as well!

Even if your children are older, if you're like almost everybody else you still have difficulty finding time to exercise. It's not something most of us get really excited about. Remember that it doesn't have to take a long time. Starting the day off with an early morning brisk walk or jog can be beneficial and give your day an energy boost. You could also buy secondhand exercise equipment, like a treadmill or step machine, to see if you like using it. (Don't spend the big bucks until you're sure you'll follow through.)

Be realistic about what your schedule will allow and start small. That way you can enjoy small successes instead of berating yourself for not fulfilling your goals!

Learning

Learning opens the mind to all the opportunities and possibilities God has given us. If you are constantly learning something new, even if it's just a new gardening technique or how to quilt, you will be a motivated, interesting person. You will also model to your children the benefits of lifelong learning. When we stop learning, we stop growing. Certainly we should all be growing spiritually and learning about the Word of God, but I think learning more about the world God gave us is also part of spiritual growth.

Maybe you disliked school, so you hate the thought of learning. Don't worry; learning is not school. Learning is approaching life with the wide-eyed wonder of a two-year-old. Nothing used to delight me more than watching my toddler chase squirrels and birds in the park. The look of pure glee in her eyes as she discovered a new creature was wonderful to watch. Many of us have lost that delight, but we can find it again.

Instead of scrolling through Facebook, read a book on a subject that interests you. If you have child care, take a continuing education class offered at night. Following is a list of subjects often offered at local colleges, shops, or clinics, or readily available through books at the library or through specialized blogs. You can add to this list based on your own interests:

- Crafts, including knitting, sewing, macramé, paper making, quilting, and others
- Gardening
- Cooking
- How to buy or sell a house
- Car maintenance
- Consumer smarts—how to get the best bargains when you shop
- Relationships—how to improve communication
- Understanding abuse—looking at the impacts of abuse on you or your friends
- Favorite historical time period—historical novels can be great for this
- Home decorating
- Child development
- Investing (I think this is very important; we'll deal with it more in chapter 9.)
- Computer skills
- Foreign languages

Relaxation

One study found that mothers on average lose 750 hours of sleep in the first year of each baby's life. If something has to be sacrificed so you can get everything done, you probably choose your own personal relaxation. Yet we all need time to refresh ourselves; that's the way God made us. Jesus, who had so many people who needed Him and so much good He could do, still withdrew from crowds to sleep, pray, or just to be with His disciples.

Many of us just don't have time for sleep, socializing, or recreation because we spend our time on the wrong things. We fear that if we relax, the baby won't get fed or the house won't get cleaned. Or we'll have nothing to feed our family for dinner. Though this way of life feels sacrificial, it is actually not loving.

Loving requires us to prioritize rest. Stephen Covey, author of *The Seven Habits of Highly Effective People*, calls these restful and renewing periods "important but not urgent."[3] They're easy to leave undone because there's no immediate effect if we don't do them. The long-term effect, though, can be grave. We can't handle even minor stresses. We are prone to spiritual attack and moral failure.[4] We blow up at our children or our husbands. We start to dislike ourselves. We need to give ourselves permission to relax. Here are some soothing ideas:

- Take a bubble bath.
- Get a haircut or a facial.
- Give yourself a manicure/pedicure.
- Do your makeup really well at least once a week.
- Take a nap.
- Read a book.
- Go to the local coffee shop.
- Go for a walk by yourself.
- Choose a hobby: knit, cross-stitch, crochet, refinish furniture, build a bookcase.
- Rearrange your furniture or give your bedroom a face-lift.

Scheduling Your New Priorities

There you go: three big picture areas that need our attention— before the iPhones, social media, or even laundry.

When your children are young, you may have to find ways to care for yourself even while you are caring for them. Perhaps you can snatch some time while they nap, or you can put on a video and claim that twenty minutes. Later, you can use time at night or when they are in school. If you work, try to use your lunch breaks and coffee breaks (if you're lucky enough to have them) to do some of these things. It's amazing how productive you can be in just fifteen minutes!

Once your life is fuller and you are focusing more on each of these elements, try increasing the amount of time and the number of things you do. But make sure that you are using some method to include the important things in your day, or you may suddenly find that a week has gone by and you have neglected something altogether!

And finding time for important things doesn't have to be onerous. Here are two ways to make sure your priorities actually get accomplished.

For More Spontaneous Moms

Make yourself some tokens: green pieces of paper for Relationship Care, yellow for Spiritual Care, and blue for Personal Care (or whichever colors work out better for you). You can even make extra tokens if you want to focus specifically on certain things.

Now make a little "To Do" box and a little "Done" box on your fridge. Every time you grab something to eat or drink, select an activity, do it, and move a token. Aim to move at least one token from each category to the "Done" box each day.

For Super-Organized Moms

Need something more meticulously organized? On Sunday night, pull out your day-planner for the week and schedule in the things you most want to get done. Then everything else—including housework—can fit around those activities.

Reap the Benefits

One of the beneficial by-products of having new priorities is that it gives us an incentive to work faster. In preparing to be a doctor, my husband had to study for about ten years straight and, needless to say, about six years into it he ran out of steam. To make himself keep going he would reward himself. Once he studied five pages in his textbook, he could read a few pages in his leisure book or play on the computer for ten minutes. This incentive made him study those five pages much more quickly! If you give yourself rewards, you will probably find yourself working both faster and happier.

SCHEDULE FOR WEEK OF:

	Sunday	Monday	Tuesday	Wednesday	Thursday	Friday	Saturday	My memory verse for this week:
7:00								
7:30								
8:00								
8:30								
9:00								
9:30								
10:00								
10:30								
11:00								SPIRITUAL CARE
11:30								1.
12:00								2.
12:30								
1:00								RELATIONSHIP CARE
1:30								1.
2:00								2.
2:30								

PERSONAL CARE

1.

2.

Shade in all the things you must do, such as work schedules, children's lessons, church meetings, and others. Then decide where you would like to schedule in your priority activities. Add housework and errands after you have already scheduled in the truly important things!

3:00						
3:30						
4:00						
4:30						
5:00						
5:30						
6:00						
6:30						
7:00						
7:30						
8:00						
8:30						
9:00						
9:30						
10:00						
10:30						
11:00						

If you are scheduling these new personal priorities, working more efficiently, and lowering some of your exhausting standards, you will probably find that you are wasting far less time in front of the computer than you did before. If you are learning new things and having more fun with your kids, housework will not take on the same importance that it once did. And as you open your mind to other possibilities, your attitudes are likely to change as housework and caring for the minutiae of life diminish in importance. Family members may be able to identify with you more, and quite frankly, find you more fun. You will be able to experience God more in your life as you concentrate on Him and open yourself up to more of the world He created.

Quick Reality Check

Choose two things from each category—spiritual care, relationship care, and personal care—that you want to pursue in the next week. Write down how you're going to do this and when. Super organized moms can use the chart on pages 82–83.

For Deeper Thought

1. Are you spending time "being still" before God? Are you allowing God to speak into your life? What steps can you take to give yourself more time with the One who loves you?

2. What do you feel is the biggest lack in your emotional life? Is it a lack of friends or a lack of time to yourself? Is it a lack of time with God? Why did things get to this point? How can you prioritize this need?

3. Are you comfortable taking care of your own needs, or does this seem selfish? Read Mark 1:35–38. When others were seeking Jesus, He still took time to be still. Can you allow yourself to do the same?

Chapter 5

Relationship U-Turns

One of my favorite Bible stories is the ten plagues. Pharaoh has everything going for him: he's in charge of Egypt; he has a workforce to build monuments to himself; he's worshipped in their religion. And in the middle of all that, God sends Moses to tell him, "Let my people go." Pharaoh isn't so keen on this idea, so God sends plague after plague until Pharaoh finally relents.

Some of the plagues are gross—like the river turning to blood—but I think the plague of the frogs is actually rather funny. Exodus 8 tells us there are frogs in Pharaoh's kneading bowls, frogs in his ovens, and frogs in his bed. The place was hopping! So Pharaoh calls Moses to ask God to get rid of them. Moses asks him, "When should I ask God?" and that's when Pharaoh says something strange. He replies, "Tomorrow" (Exod. 8:10). Not now. Later. He'd rather spend one more night with the familiar, dealing with the suffering on his own, before he lets God work. He would rather spend one more night with the frogs.

Many of us are sleeping with frogs, too—and I don't mean our husbands! I mean a lot of us are putting up with things that make us miserable because on some level that's easier than seeing God work. Think about Pharaoh: his whole worldview depended on believing that he was the Grand Poo-Bah, in charge of Egypt. If he let his slaves escape, not only was he losing his workforce; he was also acknowledging that there was a God, and that he wasn't Him. So Pharaoh waited, and tried to put up with suffering.

We often do the same thing. We are so used to things being a certain way, and so wedded to our way of seeing the world, that it's hard to imagine God stepping in and changing it. What would that look like? What would happen to my identity? What would happen to my kids? We may not like the way things are, but at some level we're comfortable with it.

And that's a problem. We've just finished looking at how we can change the way we understand our roles at home, and how we can prioritize the important things. That's all well and good. For many of us, though, change shouldn't stop there. Our problems don't just involve what we expect of ourselves or how we structure our time. They involve how we relate to our family members. If your family life has been leaving you exhausted, resentful, or feeling distant, then you need to do something about it. Instead of blaming other people, it's time to start asking, "How can I change myself?"

Throwing Off Our Burdens

That's what the writer of Hebrews was talking about in chapter 12:

> Therefore, since we are surrounded by such a great cloud of witnesses, let us throw off everything that hinders and the sin that so easily entangles, and let us run with perseverance the race marked out for us. Let us fix our eyes on Jesus, the author and perfecter of our faith, who for the joy set before him endured the cross, scorning its shame, and sat down at the right hand of the throne of God. (vv. 1–2)

Even if our days are spent driving children to Boy Scout meetings or changing diapers, we are still running the Christian race. And God tells us to "throw off everything that hinders and the sin that so easily entangles." Do you see that distinction? We can have burdens encumbering us that are not, in and of themselves, sin.

These burdens come in a variety of forms. They could be difficult workplace or school situations, financial issues, or other things, but they all sap our energy and prevent us from running full throttle for

God. But the burdens I find to be the most harmful to us are the lies we believe. We don't see things as God does. We see them through our own warped glasses.

One of the most frustrating things for a police officer when interviewing multiple witnesses to a crime is the discrepancies in what these witnesses report seeing. One witness is sure the man running away was of medium build. One is sure he was tall. Another swears he jumped into a navy car. Someone else thinks it was black. What is the true story?

When we look back on our own stories we do something similar. Instead of seeing things clearly and objectively, what we see is influenced by what happened to us before. I married a great guy who was completely and utterly committed to me, but I had a difficult time trusting him not to leave for the first few years of our marriage because I had rejection issues from childhood. It wasn't anything Keith did that was making me doubt my marriage; it was all the baggage I brought into our relationship.

If we had a permissive upbringing, we may assume that nothing is actually our fault and that someone else will always fix what goes wrong. If we were hurt by caregivers as children, we may learn not to trust people and assume that we are unlovable. For many people, getting rid of these glasses and putting on the "mind of the Lord" (1 Cor. 2:16 NRSV) needs to be first and foremost a journey of healing our past hurts. There are excellent Christian books and counselors who can help in this process. However, you don't have to wait for complete healing to be able to adopt the mind of Christ.

God tells us that we already have "everything we need for life and godliness through our knowledge of him" (2 Peter 1:3). How can that be possible if we still hurt? Because we know Christ who actually lives inside of us. The best weapon against lies is the truth. In the spiritual armor passage in Ephesians 6, truth is buckled around your waist to hold everything together. And the Word of God is the sword, fighting off the Enemy.

When we're trying to change the way we relate to those closest to us, seeing life through Christ's eyes is vitally important. Change can either be a healing force or a destructive one. Look at the difference between Martin Luther King Jr.'s peaceful resistance in his call for universal respect and the militant screams given by Malcolm X. If we want change to be a beneficial process in our families, we must keep God's perspective on human relationships. Four principles from Scripture are central to this endeavor: commitment to our families; responsibility for our choices; a servant attitude; and affirmation of others and ourselves. These help us to see clearly so that we can make changes positively rather than destructively.

Commitment to Our Families

Have you ever met a couple who you just knew was perfect for each other, but then were blown away when ten years later that marriage ended? No matter how well a marriage started, over time, couples will drift apart unless we're intentional. How you treat your spouse after you're married often has more to do with what happens to that marriage than marrying someone who is perfect (as if there were such a person).

That's why commitment matters. And commitment to the marriage doesn't just mean saying, "I'm staying 'til death do us part—even if I have to make everyone miserable in the process." It means saying, "I commit, every day, to make this marriage the best it can be." Commitment is an active, daily decision, not a one-time vow.

After all, until you can say, "I am sticking with this marriage through thick and thin," to a certain degree you will constantly be testing your husband. "Does he measure up? Is this the last straw? How much more of this will I take?" What's a guy going to do if he picks up on those cues? He's going to feel resentful and defensive, hardly ingredients for a great marriage.

Now, let me make it absolutely clear that I'm talking only about commitment in a marriage that is not abusive. If your husband is hurting you or your children, staying in the same house is definitely not necessary or even wise. But absent from abuse, adultery, or addictions, commitment means deciding to stay even if he never changes. You accept him just as he is, understanding that he is an adult who can make his own choices, whether you like them or not. This does not mean approving of his choices. You are simply acknowledging that he is ultimately accountable to God, not to you.

Commitment also means relinquishing any desire for revenge. In marriages where we women seem to do most of the giving, we often harbor bitterness toward our husband because of past wrongs—wrongs that are often very real and very painful—and at some level expect our husband to make them up to us. Yet, as marriage expert Cynthia Smith says, "Marriages only work well when both sides desist from keeping scorecards of each other's performance."[1] In 1 Corinthians 13, Paul writes that these scorecards are actually the antithesis of love.

> Love is patient, love is kind. It does not envy, it does not boast, it is not proud. It is not rude, it is not self-seeking, it is not easily angered, it *keeps no record of wrongs*. Love does not delight in evil but rejoices with the truth. It always protects, always trusts, always hopes, always perseveres. Love never fails. (vv. 4–8, emphasis mine)

Even if you don't always feel love, you can act love. Country singer Clint Black expresses this as he croons in a song he wrote for his wife: love isn't something he feels, it's something that he does. Very often it is in the very act of love that the feeling returns. Susan Page found that, though you can't change your feelings, "you can act in the presence of ambivalence."[2] When you decide to concentrate on your own behaviors instead of his, things he does may stop bothering you. You may notice the good things about your husband more, and the feeling of love may return and grow even deeper.

Finally, not being really committed to your husband can ruin any chance for your marriage to grow, because it becomes so difficult to talk about any real problems. Every time you do, the relationship itself is at stake. It's difficult to resolve long-standing issues if you're scared to even raise them with your husband!

Barriers to Commitment

This may all sound logical, but emotionally it can still be very difficult. Some of us may be wildly in love with our husbands or, at least, very happy in our marriages. Many of us, though, are not, though you would never know it to look at our families. Outwardly things look great, but inside you have nagging doubts about whether this marriage is where you're supposed to be. Maybe you have the feeling that you were somehow coerced, either by people or circumstances, into marriage or motherhood. Let's return to Diane's story for a moment. Diane was nineteen when she got pregnant. She was being pressured to abort the baby, but she didn't want to. Three months later she met Ted, who was thirty and held a stable, well-paying job, though his personal life resembled that of an eighteen-year-old. Ted latched onto Diane and enjoyed the attention that she showered upon him. He claimed her baby as his own, and they married.

It is easy to say that Diane had little choice about whether she should marry Ted. She had no money, no family support for raising her daughter, no education, and no home. Without Ted she would be on welfare with little help of ever breaking the cycle. Some of you may have been in similar situations. Pregnant before you were married, you may have felt that you had to get married in order to survive. This barrier to complete commitment can have a significant detrimental effect on your marriage. One large study found that couples who conceived a child before they were married were two times more likely to divorce than those who did not.[3]

For others of you, the circumstances may not be as clear cut. Nevertheless, you worry that you married outside of God's will. You were too young or too emotionally insecure. Maybe you were acting on the "repetition compulsion," but have woken up and realized you would never marry this same person again if you knew then what you know now.

The Problem with Leaving

There's no doubt you're in agony. Marriage should be the most satisfying relationship, and instead it causes you pain. Some of you may choose to leave, but let me give you three thoughts first.

Unless you have worked through what you are responsible for in your past and taken action to change yourself, you don't really know what your relationship can become. There's no way your marriage can stay the same if you change. Yet too often after years of not acknowledging how unhappy you are, the dam bursts and you start feeling all the resentment and anger that's built up. Your instinct is to leave. You've stuck it out this far and nothing's changed. He never will change. Why stay?

Because you haven't changed either. Maybe you're getting angry and speaking up for yourself more. But until you start dealing with the root issues that caused your marriage to get this way, you don't know what can happen!

And, if you leave at this point, statistics say you'll repeat the same mistake. That's why the divorce rate for second and third marriages is so much higher. People are already inclined to choose badly. To prevent this, you need to deal with the problems that got you here in the first place. How much better to do that while you're still in the marriage, which may then be able to be rescued!

Finally, God's grace is amazing if we accept it. He loves marriage and hates divorce. He will bless you if you stay. Research even bears this out. One long-term study of couples who characterized themselves as unhappy found that often such feelings are short-lived.[4] Five years after reporting themselves unhappily married, two-thirds of then unhappy couples were now happy. And those who stayed married were happier than those who had divorced, and even happier than those who had divorced and remarried. The problems had either disappeared, or could be dealt with because the couple decided to stay in the marriage.

Responsibility for Our Choices

Too often we blame everybody else for our unhappiness. "I'd be happy if only he'd give me some time to myself!" or "Why don't they respect me? I do everything for them and then they don't even appreciate it!" These statements reflect real feelings, but you're never going to find peace if you're saying those sorts of things to yourself.

The only way for us to grow is to hold ourselves accountable for our choices and to stop looking around at everybody else to fix our problems. Paul writes that "each of us will give an account of himself to God" (Rom. 14:12). There's no point trying to blame everyone else if we're going to have to stand before God alone someday and explain them to Him! So God warns us not to judge but to be brutally honest when we examine ourselves. The Pharisees' main problem was not that they did a whole lot of "bad" things; it was instead that they believed they were wonderful in God's sight compared to everyone else. When we focus on what we have done and not on what has been done to us, we can begin to see ourselves as capable people with choices.

Julia was only twenty-two when she divorced her husband. He had repeatedly raped and beaten her during their brief marriage. I met her when I was a teen counseling at a Christian summer camp. She was talented, vivacious, and full of life despite her trials. Most beautiful of all, she radiated peace and hope as she dealt with her pain. But, at the time, the way she was dealing with it alarmed me. She told me how she was studying the Bible with a mature Christian woman. Their focus was on Julia confessing her own sin and asking forgiveness. *How deplorable!* I thought. This woman was blaming Julia when Julia was the victim!

But looking back now, I understand the reason for the emphasis on Julia's own shortcomings. Julia sought to escape the victim role and see herself as responsible for her own actions. As a victim, Julia couldn't choose anything. But by holding Julia accountable to God, her mentor showed Julia her freedom to make choices. If we can admit we had choices in the past, we can more easily identify our choices now. And if we have choices now, then we also have the ability to change our situation.

Julia in no way claimed even close to 50 percent of the blame for the problems in her marriage. But by acknowledging where she herself had gone wrong, it was easier to leave her husband's major guilt behind. She took the focus off of him and moved it onto her own relationship with God. She was gaining freedom to grow unencumbered.

That's a lesson that more wives need to learn, because many of us are stuck in relationships that we think can never change until our husbands start doing something differently. Take my friend Diane, whose story opened this book. When she came home from the hospital the day after giving birth to her daughter, her husband, Ted, didn't make any moves to prepare dinner, so despite the pain she was feeling, Diane fixed something for the two of them. She has made all the meals ever since. One day Ted was feeling tired and sat on the couch while she brought the food to the table. He made no move to get up, so she sighed and brought his food to the couch. Now he sits there every day and waits to be served.

Diane complains that he makes her serve him everything, and she resents it very much (though she still does it). However, he never actually asked her to do these things. Quite clearly he wanted her to do them, and he was emotionally manipulating her into doing them. But Diane decided to participate in his charade. When I ask her why she continues to wait on him, she says that she doesn't want to feel guilty.

It's hard to admit that we may have played a part in our unhappiness. Perhaps you're struggling because, deep down, you feel that if you are better or more giving than your husband, then he won't reject you and leave. But in the process, you're helping to create a very unfulfilling relationship for both of you! Changing this means doing a complete U-turn in the way you view yourself.

David went through this sort of transformation when he wrote Psalm 40. God lifted him up "out of the mud and mire" (v. 2), put him on a secure foundation, and put a new song in his heart—a song of praise to God. Then David started telling everybody about it. But what really changed? If you read further into the psalm, you'll see that David was still surrounded by enemies who wanted to kill him. He was still facing the same battles.

Something had changed, but it was not his circumstances. It was his heart. Instead of crying "Why me?" he was happily saying, "I desire to do your will" (v. 8). Such a change seems impossible. Yet God gave him a new song and a new perspective on his life.

Examining Our Past Choices

Why do we spend so much time trying to fool ourselves about the reality of our lives when the Bible makes it clear (see Ps. 139) that God knows us inside out? We don't open bills because we're afraid to see how much we've carelessly spent. We don't ask our children questions about their friends because we're afraid of what we may discover. Maybe you don't want to examine your heart or to discover your true feelings, because what if you don't like what you find?

But complacency is not a valid part of the Christian life. Paul urges the Corinthians to "examine yourselves to see whether you are in the faith" (2 Cor. 13:5). Part of that examination includes seeing how past and current choices may be preventing us from experiencing true joy.

Nevertheless, some of us feel compelled to choose things that we know are wrong for us. Many of you reading this book have married men who at times are distant and perhaps uncaring. Some psychologists believe that we unconsciously choose a mate who can re-create for us the feelings we experienced while growing up, in an attempt to work through these feelings, fix things, and then feel better.[5] Sigmund Freud called this the "repetition compulsion." Psychologist and author Henry Cloud says it's similar to the biblical principle, "a dog will return to his own vomit."[6] So if we felt abandoned growing up, we may marry a workaholic. Or if we never experienced affection or affirmation, we may marry someone who has difficulty with intimacy and lives in front of the TV.

I believe that when the Bible talks about the sins of the parents being carried on to the fourth generation, part of what is being predicted is the destructiveness of inadequate parenting. A girl from a difficult upbringing often marries someone with whom she will also feel sad and so repeats the pattern for her own children. In this sense, the "passed on" sin is not just a traditional curse but instead almost a natural law of the universe.[7] If our soul is damaged, we continue to damage ourselves and our children through our poor choices. And even though God no longer punishes sin down the generations, we still have to deal with the psychological effects of bad parenting.

Examining Our Fears

The same fears that steer us to marry men who hurt us may also exacerbate our problem getting help at home. Just as Diane serves Ted his meals to avoid feeling guilty, so you may be doing more work than necessary or distancing yourself emotionally from your husband or children to avoid uncomfortable feelings. Look at the chart below and see if you identify with any of these fears.

Fear of conflict	Do you quietly seethe inside because family members don't help you, yet you haven't even talked to them about it because you're afraid of their reaction?
Fear of intimacy	Do you busy yourself with work around the house as a shield to protect yourself from having to nurture the emotional side of your relationships?
Fear of being out of control	Do you need to know everything that is going on at all times in your house to avoid feeling out of control?
Fear of taking an authority role	Do you wait and wait for your husband to be the head of the house and so don't confront him in his weak areas, or discipline the children?
Fear of losing your identity	Do you often wonder who you would be if you weren't a wife and a mother? Do you have difficulty seeing yourself primarily as a child of God? Do you define yourself by the things you do?

Acknowledging your emotional weights and bringing these before God frees you to take responsibility for proactive change in your life. Take some time to pray through some of these questions. If any of them speak to you directly, seek out a counselor to talk to or pick up some books about healing emotional pain. But above all, learn to recognize the truth and tell it to yourself several times a day. Fill your mind with truth, and you'll begin to incorporate it into your daily decisions. Then you can begin to work through these problematic ways of dealing with tension and begin to make choices freely.

A Servant Attitude

The Problem with Independence

As Christians, we are called to model Christ's servanthood. Yet some women feel threatened by the prospect of submitting their own needs to others. This is especially true for women who were abused as children. We all know women like this: after years of being the doormat they have finally found their voice, and no one is going to silence them now!

Such rugged independence is prized in the world. These people know who they are, have their lives together, and don't let people step on their toes! They're the workaholics, the control freaks, and the aggressively successful people we often try to emulate. But I can almost guarantee women like that aren't fulfilled and, probably, not even happy. Whether we like it or not, we need other people. The search for freedom can really be a personal prison. God tells us that freedom, paradoxically, is found in submitting and serving. We must learn to serve willingly if we want to receive more of God's blessing in our lives.

The Problem with Subservience

Personally, I think the main problem for women is not independence but serving inappropriately. Women have traditionally been the servants of the world, caring for their husbands, their children, and their aging relatives. Serving has become almost instinctual. This does not mean, however, that we instinctively do it right! As Mary Stewart Van Leeuwen says in her book *Gender and Grace*, one of the results of the fall is that women often struggle to hold onto a relationship, even if it means losing themselves in the process.[8] This type of serving is not the same as Christlike servanthood.

When Jesus, our example of the true servant, washed His disciples' feet, Peter tried to stop Him. He thought it was preposterous—Jesus was not his lowly servant but his master, the disciples' teacher whom they respected and loved. Jesus' servanthood was completely unexpected. That's what made it radical.

Servanthood Requires Mutual Respect

Obviously we are not Jesus and, thus, our servanthood can never be as radical. Yet there is a marked difference between Christlike servanthood and the traditional subservient role of women. It is hard to properly serve as Christ did if you are regarded as inferior to those you are serving. The sign of a first-class restaurant is that a waiter can refill your glass before you even notice you need it filled and do it in such a way that you barely notice him doing it. This is subservience. Subservience does not challenge people or aid them in understanding the character of God because the servant is doing only what he or she is expected to do.

Too often women adopt this subservient role, feeling that by sacrificing themselves to keep a nice home, they can demonstrate love to their families. Perhaps this is the root cause of your own unhappiness, because all too often it backfires and you lose the very relationships you were hoping to protect.

I recently watched an old movie called *The War at Home*, about a Vietnam vet returning to his middle-class, traditional family. Kathy Bates, portraying the mother, laments throughout the movie, "Why do you all hate me so much?" Her children and her husband never seem to do what she wants them to do, and instead find her pathetic and embarrassing. Even though she has dedicated her life to making sure there are freshly baked muffins on the table at breakfast and appropriate hymns being played at each holiday, they patronize her. She does not command respect. And it is awfully hard to love someone who you cannot respect.

I once knew a sad woman named Fatima who proved to me that even young children can be taught to disrespect their parents. Fatima attended a playgroup with me when my children were younger, and when she walked in the door, the rest of us ran for cover. She rarely disciplined her three-year-old son, Omar, so he would taunt the other children relentlessly and deliberately bait some into tantrums (especially my own precocious one). Fatima's response was to plead, "Omar, please, no." When he ignored her, she sighed and turned away. One day, while walking home with us, she was complaining about how he never listened to her. She said she wanted to be firmer, but she wanted Omar to love her, too. During this conversation, Omar was walking perilously close to the street. When he did dart out, Fatima cried, "Omar, no!" But it was me who grabbed him and brought him back. "See, I don't know what to do. He won't listen," she sighed.

Children who do not respect you when they are three will not respect you when they are fifteen. They may very well be ashamed of you or feel superior to you. They will not come to you for advice or listen to what you say because you never showed them you were serious about your own convictions. Maxine Hancock says we should think of ourselves as the servant leaders of our homes. I think by the addition of the word *leaders*, she implies that while we serve we should also command respect.[9]

Servanthood Requires Mutual Responsibility

Serving only has meaning if the person being served understands what is being done. Marie Antoinette's life is a perfect example of the problems that can ensue from inappropriate serving. She had been so pampered that she was ignorant of the realities of life. When told that the peasants had no bread, she replied, "Let them eat cake." Her nonchalant ignorant attitude eventually cost the queen her head!

Subservience gives those being served power with no responsibility. Children with a maid who hangs up discarded clothes and picks up toys will not even notice that they have made a mess. They don't even realize their actions are disrespectful because they never have had to deal with any consequences.

If we pamper our children, they will not feel responsible for their own messes, their own actions, and even more far-reaching, their own mistakes. They may grow into adults feeling a good life is owed to them without effort, or may engage in hazardous activities without thinking of what may result. If we do the same for our husbands, the chance at having a marriage relationship characterized by mutual respect and admiration is severely limited.

If your husband and children do not respect you, it will be very hard for you to model Christ to them. And modeling Jesus to your family is vitally important. If you show your children that you will always rescue them, you teach them that they are not responsible for their own lives. If they think they have no responsibility in life, they will never understand their need for salvation.

When we give people something for free, without requiring any work for it, they never have to deal with the consequences of their own actions. We always step in and save them. It's like we're putting a big roadblock between "you reap" and "you sow."[10] The fact is that we are not owed anything just because we are alive—we are not owed our life, our food, our housing, our happiness, or even our salvation. These things are all gifts, and unless your children understand that, they will never have the insight needed for true repentance.

Are You a Real Servant?

By now you're probably thinking that serving has many more repercussions than you ever dreamed! You've always served your family, but how did your efforts at serving go so wrong? And how can you tell the difference between which actions are done out of subservience and which are done from a true servant's heart?

Often the answer does not lie in what you do but in why you do it. Many who are subservient are serving to gain love and gratitude. For them serving is at heart a selfish act, even though it seems so selfless. These women make wonderful meals, clean every inch of their homes every day, and do all they can domestically to ensure that their husband and their children love them. But cleaning cannot equal love. And if we do things for people that they should rightly do themselves, they don't respect us.

The purpose of true service is to model the depth of Christ's love. It is a love that does not excuse but forgives; it sheds light on all, yet does not keep record of wrongs. A woman who serves this way is not attempting to gain love but is attempting to give it. She does what is best for the growth of her family, even if family members don't like it. Family members see that their mother is not a pushover, though she loves them. They sense why she does what she does, and they respect her for it. They don't become enmeshed in her emotional baggage but are free to explore on their own and make their own decisions.

Sometimes women are stuck in the middle. They know they need to foster responsibility, and they are not trying to gain love, but still they are not respected. They simply don't know how to organize their households in such a way as to gain respect. This is hardly surprising, since all over the world women have traditionally been of lower social standing than men. When I was on a short-term mission trip to Tunisia in North Africa, I was heartbroken by the way women were treated.

On public transit, time and again, I saw obviously weak grandmothers abdicating their seats to their healthy grandsons, or women and girls crammed in the backseats of cars while men and boys rode in front comfortably.

These situations sound outrageous to us because women in North America and Europe have made tremendous gains. That doesn't mean, though, that we're seen as of equal worth. If subservience is the only model you know, it can be hard to develop a new one.

Sometimes the attitude shift between subservience and servant leadership can best be accomplished by doing, even if you don't feel it yet. In the next few chapters, we will look at specific ways we can foster respect and accountability in our family. But first, we must look at the last attitude shift, that which impacts the core of our being: affirmation of our families and ourselves.

Affirmation of Others and Ourselves

Affirming Others

From the day I found out I was pregnant with my first child, I have not missed a day praying that my children may grow to love God and serve Him, and make decisions that will honor Him. Leading my children to develop a close relationship with God is my primary goal in parenting.

A key part of achieving a Christlike attitude of servanthood and commitment to our families is affirming who they are before God, regardless of how this reflects on you or how you feel about it. Affirmation means always recognizing that this person, be it your husband or your child, is created in the image of God, even if he or she has physical, emotional, or intellectual habits that drive you up the wall! No matter our weaknesses, God loves us all so much that He says He has engraved us "on the palms of [His] hands" (Isa. 49:16).

When the ultrasound picked up my son's heart defect, and further tests detected Down syndrome, we were counseled by physicians, friends, and even some family members to abort. We did not. During the twenty-nine days he spent on this earth, he taught us more about life and about God than any other human being has. God gave him to us with his physical limitations, and we loved him through it all.

Most of you will never be asked to love like that. Usually we reject family members not due to illness but because they do not live up to our expectations. Often we expect them to be just like us, and when they're not, clashes occur.

Robin Norwood, author of *Women Who Love Too Much*, uses the example of "Beauty and the Beast" to show the benefits of true affirmation. Most people, she says, believe that the fairy tale goes something like this: A beautiful woman meets a beast. She loves him, and through that love she changes him. Norwood points out, though, that Beauty doesn't ask the Beast to change. She loves him for who he is without ever expecting anything else. "Because of her attitude of acceptance, he [is] freed to become his own best self." She goes on to say,

> True acceptance of an individual as he is, without trying to change him through encouragement or manipulation or coercion, is a very high form of love, and very difficult for most of us to practice. At the bottom of all our efforts to change someone else is a basically selfish motive, a belief that through his changing we will become happy. There is nothing wrong with wanting to be happy, but to place the source of that happiness outside ourselves, in someone else's hands, means we avoid our ability and responsibility to change our own life for the better.[11]

Affirmation is loving a person as God gave him to you. Imagine if cloning takes off and future generations can determine their children's personalities and talents. If we all created superchildren, wouldn't the world be boring? God creates variety because He loves it, and He makes it an intrinsic part of the human condition. Let's praise God that He looks to the heart and loves everyone. At the end of one of our favorite VeggieTales videos, Bob the Tomato says, "Remember, God made you special, and He loves you very much." A good lesson for us all.

Affirming Ourselves

Believing your children and your husband are special may be easier for you than believing that you are special. For a healthy family unit and personal inner peace, though, it is vital that our affirmation also be directed inward. Some women just don't feel that they deserve very much. We beat ourselves up for our inadequacies. It's time to start filling our minds with truth: To God, you are precious and irreplaceable, the temple of the Holy Spirit Himself.

Other women may be miserable because they find their identity in suffering. They are proud of their misery, as it gives them a way to feel superior to others and keep them in debt. It is not, however, a debt that they want canceled. Even though they are truly miserable, they have a hard time changing because suffering for others is the only way they know how to relate to others.

Rob is now in his thirties with a wonderful family. His wife had a difficult upbringing, and Rob has patiently and lovingly helped her work through many of her issues. Yet he reacts in frustration and anger when she is unhappy and he can't help. He always feels he must do something, even if she feels she needs to be sad for a while.

Rob attributes much of his frustration to the way he interacted with his mother. Though she devoted herself to her family, she always made it clear how much she had sacrificed for them. Whenever he or his sisters wanted to go out, she would say, "Go, have fun. I'll just stay here by myself, like always. I have so much to do anyway." If anyone did try to help her, she would say, "I've always done this by myself. I don't know why you are helping now." Rob felt that he was responsible for his mother's misery growing up. Now he feels Susan's problems are his to fix, even when Susan wants to work through them alone.

Rob's mother was miserable. She did too much of the housework; she received little help; she resented it. A woman who actively plays the martyr for the family will have a hard time changing. She will hang onto her misery like a life preserver.

Unfortunately, some Christian groups attract those who are acting the martyr role. When I was sixteen I participated in a summer mission program. That summer our motto was "The way up is down." Almost all of our Bible studies focused on how God blesses those who are in dire circumstances. Our team's project was to build a kindergarten in a large Third World city. When a delivery van came to unload the gravel that we needed to mix into the cement, the head leader told him to dump it in the pile of sand that had already accumulated near the gate. When the worker said he could just as easily dump it on a bare piece of asphalt where it would be easier to use, the leader said the team members could pick the pebbles out individually, to learn patience and discipline.

While patience and discipline are important Christian virtues, I do not believe that the need for them necessitates creating our own suffering. Very often we feel God's grace more acutely when we are suffering, as my husband and I did during our son's illness and after his death. To create such circumstances, though, is to neglect the blessings that God wants to give us. Many times we have difficulty receiving from others because we worry that we might then be in someone's debt. But the result is that we're not allowing ourselves to experience love, and we are not allowing those we love most the opportunity to express it!

How would you feel if your preschooler came up to you and said, "No matter how much it makes me smile or makes me laugh, I never want you to hug or tickle me again"? Or if your teenager told you that she never wanted you to have heart-to-heart talks with her when she's down? In all likelihood, you would be heartbroken. Yet I think this is what we are doing when we try to create our own suffering. There are obviously spiritual blessings found in fasting for a time, but what makes it effective is that it has a time limit. If you are living a life where you are constantly emotionally fasting, Paul warns that you are neglecting much of the gospel. Colossians 2:18 says, "Do not let anyone who delights in false humility . . . disqualify you for the prize." He is referring to people who create rules about things but ignore the blessings that come from being connected to Christ. He ends by telling us to let Christ lead our lives, not our rules and regulations.

Too many of us are attracted to this "sufferers" version of Christianity. We internalize this partial Christian message—that God is close to those who suffer—and turn it around on ourselves because it fits with our own perceptions of what we deserve. Affirmation, on the other hand, means recognizing that God does not require you to suffer in every area of your life. God is the loving Father who longs to give good gifts to His children (Luke 11:13).

Quick Reality Check

Let's bring ourselves to God in prayer. Like David did, ask God, "Search me, O God, and know my heart; test me and know my anxious thoughts. See if there is any offensive way in me, and lead me in the way everlasting" (Ps. 139:23–24). Ask Him to gently reveal where you need forgiveness, freedom from bitterness, anger, or shame.

For Deeper Thought

1. Luke 9:62 says, "No one who puts his hand to the plow and looks back is fit for service in the kingdom of God." Are there things in your past that are calling, or regrets that haunt you today? Pray that you will be able to give these to God and concentrate on the plans He has for you now (Jer. 29:11).

2. Read prayerfully Romans 12:9–21. See how God wants us to act toward each other. Ask God where you need to concentrate on improving and pray for Him to help with this.

Chapter 6

The Family That Cleans Together

You're working on a schedule. You're cleaning quickly to music. You're spending time on what's truly important. There's only one problem: there still aren't enough hours in the day! You're still overwhelmed by how much there is to do, and now that you're expanding your horizons, you want even more time for these important things. The time has come to ask for help.

If you do this while remembering the principles of positive change—responsibility, commitment, servanthood, and affirmation—then you'll probably succeed in making your family life better. I know this sounds far-fetched; after all, how can asking for help improve your family? They'll grumble and complain, or just refuse. But if you ask in the right way, without trying to punish them, you'll probably end up with a stronger marriage and more mature children.

Research shows that families who clean together are actually stronger. If God declared that the right way to organize families was to let the woman do all the housework and child care, whether or not she also worked outside the home, then we should expect families with a strict division between women's work and men's work to be the healthiest. Yet research shows the opposite.

Let's look at the effect on kids first. At its most basic, children fare better when they see Dad scrubbing pots. They also show marked improvement on all psychological tests when dads take time with them. Sociologist Scott Coltrane found that "children whose fathers don't share responsibilities for the everyday details of their upbringing, had lower intellectual, cognitive, social, and emotional skills than children whose fathers shared work with their mothers."[1]

Turning to men, a huge 2012 Western European study on gender and housework found that the more housework a man did, the happier he tended to be. Conflict in marriage went down, and happiness of both partners went up.[2] If we turn to women, we'll find that they're also emotionally stronger in families where work is shared. Women who stay at home and do most household chores experience higher levels of stress than any other group of women in society.[3] And perhaps not surprisingly, marriages are breaking up because of it. In a large-scale study of the causes of divorce, Joan Huber and Glenna Spitze found that more wives than husbands reported contemplating divorce, and they had done so largely because of "their resentment of having the lion's share of household tasks."[4] Basically, the more helpful the husband, the less likely the wife is to consider divorce. We can even quantify this. For every daily household task that hubby performs at least 50 percent of the time, the wife is 3 percent less likely to contemplate divorce.[5]

Obviously, then, the housework itself is not the cause of our problems. The problems seem to have more to do with our relationship patterns surrounding housework than with the work itself. Housework is done within the family, so it affects the relationships within that family. And when women do most of the work, housework can have a detrimental effect on the family. We need to stop thinking about housework as the woman's problem; it's really the family's job. Of course, there will be some families in which the woman does all the housework but the relationships do not suffer. But according to the large-scale studies of housework patterns, these are the exception. So if sharing housework can help our relationships, it's time to consider spreading the load. Let's look at our candidates for housework help.

The Candidates

Your Children

Most women agree that children are valid candidates for household help, especially given the amount of mess they create! I remember finding with glee Proverbs 10:5, which says, "a child who gathers in summer is prudent, but a child who sleeps in harvest brings shame" (NRSV). Children should participate in the work of the family. They shouldn't get free rides! It's important that kids learn the responsibility and basic skills that come from doing housework. And the best gift you can give your future daughter-in-law is a son who cleans toilets!

Your Husband

Husbands, however, are a different story entirely. You have no authority over them, and you can't—and shouldn't—insist they help you. Besides, it may not always be appropriate that they do help. Perhaps your husband already does a lot of work around the house—just not housework. Paul and Aimee bought a fixer-upper house because they didn't want to be saddled with huge debt. In his free time, Paul works on the house to improve it. Aimee doesn't know how to do these fixing-up jobs, so she leaves them for Paul and does the housework herself. They both contribute to making and keeping the house livable.

When my husband was in his residency and working truly ridiculous hours, I felt that it was better for me to do most of the housework. I wanted him to spend the little time he did have at home having fun with his family rather than worrying about grocery shopping or whether he was doing his share of the vacuuming.

My friend Derek also works crazy hours. He can be absent from home for more than twelve hours a day during his busy season. Lisa, his wife, is quite happy to do the work of keeping the house together because he's so exhausted she feels it's only fair. She also wants to give him a break when he does get home. When they go camping, though, he makes a point of doing the dishes and other mundane tasks because, as he puts it, "It's her turn for a break now."

For many women, however, the reason they may feel it's inappropriate to ask for help has little to do with actual work arrangements and everything to do with role expectations. Many women, even some of those who also work outside the home, feel they should be the ones solely responsible for the housework. Even though they are doing what is traditionally men's work, they don't think it's right for men to do what is traditionally women's work. There are no easy answers for this dilemma, except to say that God is always more interested in your spiritual condition than in the condition of your home. Ask yourself if your current arrangement best glorifies God within your family. If not, maybe it's time to recruit some help!

Too often, though, women feel burdened by housework not because of their own expectations of their roles but because of their husband's expectations. I remember one morning at Bible study my friend Shelly was livid at her husband's attitude toward the house. She had spent the previous day caring for two children under two, dealing with a repairman, taking the kids to playgroup, making sure everyone had lunch, doing all the laundry, and then making dinner. She had no time or energy to clean, and when her husband came home, the living room was in chaos. As soon as he walked in the door, he said, "What happened here?" and proceeded to inform her that she'd have to try harder because he couldn't live like this. Shelly blew up, feeling like he was asking too much of her.

My own marriage has often been plagued with these sorts of disagreements, since I put more value on creativity and play than tidiness, and Keith likes order. But whether the problem is that you don't expect him to work, or that he expects you to work much harder than you do, you can still find a common goal: a welcoming house with a degree of order. If you've concluded that either your husband or your kids are candidates to help you achieve this goal, here's how you can recruit their labor.

How to Convince Them You Need Help

One of your biggest hurdles to getting help from your family can be that they don't believe you really need or want it. After all, if you saw your husband constantly doing one thing, unable to sit still until he was finished, and obsessively thinking and talking about it, would you think he was doing something he enjoyed? Even if he complained about it? Men may not believe that you're serious when you complain because they complain for different reasons. Psychologist John Gray, author of the famous *Men Are from Mars, Women Are from Venus*, says that men often complain so they can feel in control. But on some level, they really enjoy what they're doing, because they get a reward from doing it, something maybe as simple as a sense of being needed. The complaint is a cover to allow them to vent the conflicting feelings.[6] If they honestly didn't want to do something, they probably wouldn't do it. So men may assume that if you truly didn't want to do something, you wouldn't do it either, except in rare or temporary circumstances.

Children probably think the same way. They don't do things they don't want to do unless someone is making them, and they think, as a parent, who can make you do anything? So when your husband and your children hear you complain about how much work you do, they probably don't understand how serious you are. No one would spend that much time on something they hated, would they?

How do we get our family to understand that we would appreciate some help? We can ask appropriately, and we can take action. In the rest of this chapter, we'll focus on the former.

Asking Appropriately

Don't Nag

First let's talk about how not to ask for help. The first big no-no is nagging. It's annoying, it's degrading, and it never works anyway. Nagging lets us vent our frustrations, so we feel like we've made the situation better—even if we haven't. And it gives our children and our husbands justification for not helping. (Who would want to help someone who's always "on their case"?)

Maybe you can identify with this common scenario (and anyone who knows me will recognize my family here): you go down to the basement to do the laundry, and as you descend the stairs you see that the children have strewn every toy they own across the floor in an attempt to find something. The cushions are off the couch and are currently being used to make a spaceship. The dress-up clothes are hanging from every surface in the room. You go ballistic. You yell things like, "How many times have I told you to pick up your own things? This is not fair! Do you expect me to clean all of this for you?" Your kids roll their eyes and make some halfhearted attempt to put something away. As soon as you're gone they resume playing. When you descend yet again to switch loads in the dryer, you find nothing has changed, and you yell even more.

What is the result? Does the basement get cleaned? I know that more often than not you end up doing most of the picking up. Meanwhile, you feel guilty for yelling, and the children feel insulted that you treated them that way. They don't want to help; they're angry with you. Sometimes we get so frustrated that we yell, or harp on our children whenever they come into view. We are trying to maintain the illusion that we actually have some control. But natural as it may feel, this is not the route to take if you want things to change.

It is also the very antithesis of how we should be treating each other. Ephesians 4:29 says, "Do not let any unwholesome talk come out of your mouths, but only what is helpful for building others up according to their needs, that it may benefit those who listen." Our words should build others up. Nagging and yelling destroy the spirit; asking honestly and appropriately does not.

A similar dynamic is at work with husbands. While we may not yell at them in the same way we do our children, we may snap at them, or even helpfully—in our minds—remind them of the task they promised to do. This makes them more likely to dig in their heels and not do whatever it may be, wanting to retain their self-respect. They don't want to give in to nagging—and nor should they. When we stop nagging and start communicating with respect, family members are more likely to take us seriously and make an effort to help us.[7]

Host a Family Meeting

Even if we can agree that nagging is wrong, what does the alternative look like? It does not mean that we go through life doing nothing but praising others. It does mean, however, that we should be honest and look out for others' best interests. One of the most effective ways to do this with regard to housework is to show your family the big picture, then let them be a part of the solution. If you have never discussed the family workload as a group before, why not try? Even children as young as four or five can understand that some jobs need to be done and that someone needs to do them. Open their eyes to how much work there is in keeping the house, and they may empathize more with you and volunteer for some duties. Kathy Peel, in her book *The Family Manager*, suggests talking your family through a room-by-room tour of the house, asking them to list what jobs need to be done in each room, and how often.

Now here's where you have to be careful. Instead of using the meeting to dictate what you believe needs to be done, use it as a problem-solving session, trying to give them all an opportunity to own the housework issue and work out a fair solution. You must be willing to bend your standards, too. You may believe the kitchen floor needs to be mopped twice a week, while everyone else feels once a week is OK. If you want them to participate, give in on some of these points!

One other potential roadblock: don't just list the jobs that you're frustrated with. List everything that goes into making a home run—even if there are jobs that your husband has been doing, to little fanfare of his own. Maybe he always mows the grass, or takes the car in for an oil change, or does the finances. List these things, too. When all the tasks are in front of you, in black and white, his contribution may be more obvious.

Once you've all decided what needs to be done, start asking for volunteers. Decide what's fair for each child to do. Some families say one major chore a week for each year of life (after age 5); some leave certain rooms for each child. Others tie chores with allowances, which we will discuss in the next chapter. Talk to your family about what you all think is fair, and then try to allocate the jobs. I've included an amended monthly chore schedule (see page 112), with a column for the name or initials of the person assigned each chore. Once they see how many have "Mom" written beside them, they may start to realize how much you really do and how unfair it is when they do not contribute!

Ask Your Husband for Help

Ideally, a family meeting will inspire cooperation from everybody. For some, though, family meetings won't be enough. Some husbands may not even agree to have one. You may have to start at a more rudimentary level: asking for help for individual chores. This can often be a stumbling block for many women, because we don't want to ask. They should already know we need help. When Rose broke her foot in

Chore to be done	Name	Week 1						Week 2						Week 3						Week 4					
		M	T	W	T	F	S	M	T	W	T	F	S	M	T	W	T	F	S	M	T	W	T	F	S
DAILY																									
WEEKLY																									
MONTHLY																									

a car accident, she found walking difficult. Her husband and teenage daughters, who were used to having their meals prepared, started fending for themselves. But nobody thought to get Rose anything. For two weeks she subsisted on soup, toast, and bananas. She later complained how inconsiderate they all were. "But, Rose," her husband, Howard, said, "you never asked."

Perhaps you are in the opposite camp. Maybe you have talked until you were blue in the face, but still your husband never lends a hand. In both cases, it's clear that there's a communication breakdown.

Make Your Needs Known

You cannot expect your husband to help you unless you first tell him you need help.[8] Do you have a problem making your needs known? If you and your husband never fight, perhaps you do. Fighting, of course, is never something to strive for, but it is a common by-product when two imperfect people try to merge. A lack of disagreements could indicate that you never ask for help or never confront your husband about problems.

Do you remember Diane, whose husband, Ted, never lifted a finger? Until recently they had never fought. Because of the inequities in their relationship, she seethed inside. She was afraid of conflict. She had such a disruptive childhood that even the threat of conflict felt worse than having to deal with her day-to-day frustrations.

Maybe you, too, have never talked to your husband about the things that are bothering you. Women are famous for saying, "Well, if you don't know, I'm not going to tell you." Yet is this reasonable? He is not, after all, you. Let's own our feelings and then share them. I am not advocating fighting; but learning how to constructively air feelings is an important step in promoting the intimacy we all need.

Let Your Husband Be Himself

Men will be defensive if we try to turn them into copies of us, and reject what is essentially "them." Too often we expect our husbands to act as we would. When confronted with a mess that we're tired of cleaning, we may vow to ourselves, "Fine. I'll leave the dishes there until you feel like doing them," as if this will magically get them scrubbed.

But think about how your husband lived before he married you. Did he live at home where his mother did the dishes? Did he live with other bachelors where the dishes piled up? Did he live alone and only eat pizza? If your husband lived in a pigsty before, it is likely that his tolerance for mess is considerably higher than yours. So testing him to see when (or if) he will clean is unlikely to work. Communicate your expectations and come to a solution you both like.

Let Him Know He's Needed

The best way to reach a solution is to help your husband understand that you need him. When you take charge of everything at home, and especially everything with the children, your husband may feel that he's not needed. Many biblical commentators think that the meaning of "the husband is the head of the wife" in Ephesians 5:23 implies something similar to "source," like the head of the river. The wife draws energy and support from her husband, and the husband finds part of his identity in supplying his wife with what she needs. If we, as women, strive to become completely self-sufficient, we deprive our husbands of something they need to fulfill their God-given role. They will feel distant, perhaps like a failure, or as if something is missing, even if they don't know what it is. We also rob ourselves of the gift of being cared for.

To encourage this symbiotic relationship, focus on what he already does that you need and appreciate. The top of this list is usually his work outside the home. We don't often think to thank him for this contribution—it seems so obvious. But let him know you depend on him, you understand how hard he works for the family, and that you appreciate it. Then take the opportunity to show him he's needed at home, too. Often men feel superfluous at home, like they don't even belong, because you manage everything. Make honest requests of him that allow him to help support you and feel involved in building your home.

Asking, though, should be a specific request for help, and not a test of his love or his desirability as a husband. Turn a request into a test, and he'll sense that and react defensively. Making an honest request means giving him the freedom to say no.

In fact, if you feel the temptation to reject him if he refuses, you could be skating on thin ice with your attitude. The Bible calls for wives to submit to their husbands (Eph. 5:22). This doesn't require blind obedience, but it does mean that we should consider his needs before our own. Of course, he is similarly asked to do this for us, in Ephesians 5:21, but nowhere does it say that we only have to submit if he does it first!

Part of this submission, I think, is trusting God to do the work to change his heart. We shouldn't charge in with a hammer, trying to pound away at our husband's faults. We should stand back—or rather, kneel down—and pray for God to slowly chip away at these faults in His perfect time. If we demand changes of our husband, we're not submitting. We're barging in on territory that's not ours, and we could be jeopardizing God's refining work in the process.

That doesn't mean, though, that we can't change how we act, nor does it mean that we have to acquiesce to every request he makes (as I explained in the last chapter in the section on servanthood, and talk more about in the next chapter). But it does mean that we can't try to control him; that's not submitting, that's not loving, and that's not right.

If you do give him the right to say no, not only are you leaving God room to work, you're also changing the dynamic of your relationship. Since you are no longer rejecting him, you may find that he changes how he relates to you in return. So whether he agrees to help or not, stay affectionate and don't complain. This way, you build up positive goodwill for your next request.[9] And if you appreciate him when he does do something—even if it's something you've been doing unappreciated for years—he's more likely to help you again. Men thrive on appreciation; if you appreciate them, they will probably help more.[10]

Make Your Requests Specific

The way we phrase our requests can go a long way in determining whether they will be honored. When asking for help, be brief and very specific. Men generally don't like having to interpret what we want, though women may be very used to reading between the lines. Being specific helps men to avoid feeling as if they are being attacked. Most men are very sensitive to any perceived "guilt trips," even when we are not intending them.

When we women ask for something, we tend to justify our request to show that we are not being selfish in our asking. This works fine with other women, but for men it might backfire. For instance:

USUAL REQUEST	HOW HE INTERPRETS IT	HOW YOU CAN REPHRASE IT
Honey, there's no milk and the children need to have cereal in the morning. Can you just run out and get some?	How could you not know that your children need to eat cereal? Don't you notice anything about them? How could you have taken the last of the milk? Why haven't you already left to get it?	Would you mind running out and getting some milk?
The faucet's leaking again. I don't know how to fix it, and it's driving me crazy. Can you fix it before the weekend?	Why didn't you fix it right the first time? How could you even imagine you could go out with friends and leave me and the kids here this weekend with a leaky faucet?	Would you mind fixing the faucet tonight?
Honey, can you help with dinner? The baby's pulling at my leg, and I'm finding it really hard to get everything done. If you can give me just ten minutes, we can probably eat a little quicker.	How can you just sit there when the baby is bothering me while I'm trying to make your food? Don't you care about us? Are you totally lazy?	Would you mind peeling the vegetables? (Many don't know how to "help with dinner." You have to be specific.)

Delegate Appropriately for Him

If you want your husband to take responsibility for certain chores on his own, without being asked, you need to find a delegation method that conveys to him what needs to be done without threatening him. Below are some suggestions. Sit down and talk to him about them and choose the ones that work best with your husband's personality.

Lists

My husband is motivated by lists. If I just tell him I would like him to help clean up after dinner, he doesn't know what to do. But if there is a list of daily and weekly chores on the fridge, and he can see what is left to be done, he's like a Tasmanian devil whirling around the house, cleaning.

Lists can serve a variety of purposes. If your husband doesn't understand what you do all day, having a list on the fridge of every chore that you do can help him realize that you do indeed work. For some people, having lists of his and her jobs can be helpful. He can then actually see that he is behind. This is the way many men function at their jobs, and for some it may also be an effective motivator at home.

Choices

For others, lists are debilitating. They would rather be given a choice or a range of tasks needing to be done. Some women I know tell their husbands that there are ten big jobs they would appreciate having completed soon. The men are then free to pick whichever one or two they want to accomplish at that time.

Areas of Ownership

Some men prefer having one or two big areas of responsibility. Maybe your husband can be the one who always does the dishes or who always bathes the children. If the task is always his responsibility, he is more likely to do it. It is also easier to figure out whether he is living up to his part of the bargain, or whether a new solution needs to be found.

Remove Impediments to His Work

Finally, some men are perfectionists and dislike trying to work where children can get underfoot. Maybe your husband won't help clean because the children are around. If you take the kids out for a walk for half an hour (it's amazing how much you can get done when there are no children around), he may suddenly become Mr. Clean.

Stand Back and Be Quiet!

Once you have used these methods to encourage your husband and children to participate in caring for the house, it is vitally important that you refrain from criticizing, hovering, helping, or making suggestions of how to do the task better. All these things are self-defeating. If you criticize your husband's efforts at housework, you are telling him he is incompetent, and he is less likely to try again. He'd rather do things he's good at![11]

The same dynamic is at work when our little ones try to master a task. Give them the freedom to learn and make mistakes, or they will feel like you are rejecting them, not just the work they are doing.

Another harmful thing we can do is step in when the others complain about having to do chores. Some family members may sulk because they instinctively know that we women have a hard time handling it. If you have the fortitude to wait it out, the sulking usually subsides. If you step in, you are denying them the right to have their feelings.[12]

Children are perhaps the most blatant grumblers. They don't just complain; they sigh, drag themselves around the room, and even whimper. When my youngest daughter was four, her preferred method of cleaning up the dress-up clothes was to melodramatically fall to the floor and pull herself along as if she were crawling in the desert, dying of thirst. But the clothes did get put away! If you can't stand the grumbling and the theatrics, leave the room. And don't attack them for it, as long as they are getting the assigned task done.

Why do we so often shoot ourselves in the foot by doing these things? I believe it reflects the ambivalence we feel about asking for help. Because how we feel about ourselves is usually so wrapped up in the condition of our homes, we are often reluctant to relinquish control of housework, even if we genuinely dislike doing all of it ourselves. If you find yourself on the verge of stepping in, stop and remind yourself of these points:

1. Positive reinforcement is a better motivator than criticism. If you praise your family, even if the job is not done as well as you would do it, they are more likely to take pride and ownership of the task and want to master it.

2. People need practice. Expecting immediate perfection is unfair.
3. The goal is to get them to do the task, not to control their feelings. They do not have to miraculously like to do the dishes, nor must they refrain from complaining, unless they're being rude or disruptive. If they see that complaining gets them nowhere, they'll likely stop doing it.
4. You are doing your children a favor by teaching them skills and responsibility. If you back down, you could do them harm.
5. Your husband needs to feel that he is helpful to you. If you criticize or suggest changes, you're communicating disrespect. He may feel that you believe he is incompetent, and that you don't appreciate him, and then he is more likely to give up.

There may, however, be times when the job isn't done properly. Perhaps it was Susie's turn to clean the bathroom. She's run a cloth over the bathtub, but it's still coated with scum. Bring her in and find things you can honestly praise. "Look how clean you got the mirror! There are no streaks at all!" Tell her she's getting better, but that she needs to get the scum off the bathtub. Then make sure she knows how to do it properly.

With husbands, remember that your role is not to criticize but to simply communicate your concerns. Wait for a peaceful time and ask if you can talk about some concerns you're having. Let him know how you're feeling, then ask if he thinks your assessment is fair. Listen to him and make sure you're not being too stringent. Ask for input on how you're doing, too, and then he'll feel less like you're attacking him and more like you're working together toward a common goal. Perhaps there are things he'd like you to help him with, too, like paying the bills, making sure the car gets regular maintenance, or other tasks. Above all, approach your husband with humility. If you want help around the house, it's because you want it to be shared, and that means you're not in charge. You're not setting the standards; you are setting them together, so his opinion matters as much as yours does.

Give up nagging and yelling and learn to ask appropriately. This will likely go a long way toward getting you some help. For some of us, though, this solution doesn't go far enough. The issue isn't only getting them to help us, it's making sure we stop helping them inappropriately. In this respect, asking may not be enough. You may need to take action. And that's where we'll turn in the next chapter.

Quick Reality Check

1. Think about whether your husband has the time to help you with housework. How much time does he have apart from his work outside the home? What does he do around the house already? Is he an appropriate candidate to help you?

2. What is your attitude about children helping around the house? Do you believe they should do chores? Have you been able to put this belief into practice? Read Ephesians 6:1–3. What is your role in helping your children receive this promise?

For Deeper Thought

1. When you talk to your husband and children, do you build up or tear down? Try not to nag, complain, or criticize at all today, even if you think other people deserve it. Let a few days go by and then try some of the techniques for asking appropriately. Memorize Ephesians 4:15.

2. Can you handle help? What will happen if the bathroom isn't as clean as you would like it? Can you let go of the tasks and allow others to master them?

Chapter 7

Don't Just Sit There— Do Something!

*A*bout a decade ago I watched an episode of *Oprah*, during which a woman described how her husband always left his dirty underwear strewn across the bedroom floor. She had tried everything to get him to pick them up. She had used every kind of hamper available; she had positioned these hampers in the bathroom, by the bed, and in the hall; she had left the lid up and the lid down; but still he refused to pick up his underwear. One day she got so fed up that she threw all his underwear out. The next day all he had was some ratty boxer shorts with holes in them.

Everyone on the show was asking the question, "How can she get him to pick up his underwear?" But I think that's the wrong starting point. The more important question is, "Why is she picking them up in the first place?"

It is a wonderful gift you can give your husband to create a comfortable home for him, especially if he's working hard to support the family. Doing little things for him—including picking up his underwear—can be a real blessing and a labor of love. I do little things like this for my husband, and he appreciates it. He does little things for me, too!

In a relationship like that, picking up underwear seems so trivial. Who cares who gets the underwear to the hamper? But in a relationship like Diane's, where Diane is working off her feet, where they have little intimacy, and where Diane feels completely taken for granted, the underwear matters. It has become a symbol of the fact that he won't do even the most basic of things for himself. He's learning to treat her with disrespect. It's not underwear that's the issue, then.

It's not the underwear that matters, then. It's the dynamic of the relationship. Geri Scazzero, in her book *The Emotionally Healthy Woman*, puts it like this: far too often women overfunction in the relationship. We take on tasks that are not ours to own. And by doing that, we cause others to underfunction, which isn't good for them, either. They learn not to take personal responsibility, not to think of others, and not to take initiative. If you are overfunctioning, then it's quite likely that someone else—your husband, your kids, or both—are underfunctioning. And eventually something's gotta give, because you can't overfunction forever. You'll get tired, and, like this woman with the underwear-dropping husband, you'll grow resentful.

In this chapter, we will look at what is reasonable for us to do ourselves, how we do these things while still commanding respect, and how we can encourage our family members to accept some household responsibilities. We've already talked about changing the way we ask. Now let's talk about changing our actions. Scazzero describes the process like this: "You admit you are overfunctioning and are now ready to disrupt the status quo. The rules of the relationship are about to change. . . . It is not telling someone else what to do; it is telling them what you are going to do or not do."[1] You're going to start giving people incentives to work, and instituting consequences when they don't. And in the process, you'll be creating a much healthier family dynamic.

Step 1: Incentives

Allowances for Children

When my oldest daughter turned three, she entered a new stage in her life. I was getting sick and tired of constantly picking up her toys. I decided that if she was old enough to throw them out of the toy box, she was old enough to put them back in. We started a chart of "Family Jobs," listing her chores: putting away her toys three times a day; brushing her teeth; and carrying her laundry basket to the laundry area. Every time she finished a job, she brought me a crayon and we drew a happy face on her chart. At her next birthday, we instituted "Money Jobs." After she completed four weekly tasks, she received an allowance.

I had prepped her for these new tasks by encouraging her to help me mop, dust, clean, or whatever else I was doing, even when she was very young. She thought it was fun, and I nurtured that enthusiasm. Sometimes she slowed me down, but at the age of three, she could dust a coffee table by herself, and today, at the age of seven, she can clean the whole bathroom. Now she is saving me time!

Neale Godfrey, in her book *A Penny Saved*, talks about the importance of teaching children about both money and community responsibility.[2] She encourages parents to start work for pay when children turn three, with jobs tailor-made for small ones. Then, as kids age, you can add chores. Here's what I would consider age-appropriate chores:

Age 3–4	Put toys away in toy bins. Dust a coffee table. Clean the outside of the stove and the bottom of the fridge. Dust baseboards. Get dressed by yourself (Mommy lays out clothes).
Age 5	Brush teeth by yourself (especially with an egg timer there). Start putting dishes in the dishwasher. Choose your own clothes. Clean walls/cupboards/doors with water and a cloth.
Age 6	Make your own bed. Sort socks. Sort your own laundry by whites and colors (empty your hamper into the laundry room).
Age 7	Dry dishes. Put your own laundry away after Mom folds it.
Age 8	Clean room by yourself. Tidy anywhere in the house. Clean a bathroom (including the toilet). Wash dishes while standing on a stool (not necessarily pots yet). Pack for yourself if you're going away. Pack your lunch for school.
Age 9	Wash dishes. Fold laundry. Make cookies by yourself, and cake from a mix.
Age 10	Put a load of clothes in the washing machine. Mop a floor.
Age 11	Vacuum. Make three different meals (spaghetti, chicken pie, ham, for instance). Supervise younger siblings by yourself.
Age 12	Babysit. Sort out the organization of your own room, or a linen closet, or a front hall.

As children grow, tasks can grow progressively more difficult. I give my daughters one task per year of age per week. To receive their allowance, they must complete all the tasks. This teaches them that they have to do the whole job, not just a part of it. And the "Family Jobs" are not optional—they must be done before the "Money Jobs."

Money and Responsibility

This system has the added benefit of teaching children to handle money. Godfrey advises giving children an allowance of $1 for each year of age. This may sound like a lot—especially if you have an eight-year-old, an eleven-year-old, and a teen. But you can ask older children to absorb expenses like clothes, entertainment, special trips, Christmas gifts, or other things you deem appropriate. It might actually save you money in the long run! This way, you don't just give your children money to do with whatever they want; you also teach them how to handle it. Godfrey's system, which we have adapted in our home, requires the kids to split their money between three jars: Long-Term Savings, Short-Term Savings (usually for purchases taking a few weeks to save for), and Spend Now (usually on candy, if your children are like mine!). I added a fourth jar for tithing. As children age, you can expand the jar system. If you use one system consistently, by the time your children graduate high school, they will have well-ingrained savings habits, discriminating spending habits, and a nest egg for college. When my oldest left for university last fall, she had already saved enough for two years of schooling. "I can't believe you gave me a university jar at age 3!" she laughed. But she's got the bank account to show for it.

Even if your children are older and you have never instituted any sort of regular chores, it is not too late to start. They may protest. But if you are firm about their need to work for pay, they will probably give in just to get their allowance.

An added benefit of this system is that it gets your children to help you with the housework without having to nag or get frustrated with them. Once children are old enough to read they'll know what they have to do and when. You just need to leave them alone to do it. If they don't, they will learn the consequences (no allowance). You won't have to yell or make a scene with them because you will have already explained what happens when they don't do their chores. Consequences, not lectures, teach your children. And they're much easier on your nerves.

For this to really be effective, you need to make earning money attractive. If you buy your children chocolate bars or new toys whenever you're at the store, you leave them nothing to buy for themselves! But if they know they won't get that candy, or that Barbie, or that new pair of designer jeans unless they work for it, they'll pick up that dusting rag much more eagerly.

Another incentive method you can use, especially with younger children, is to make chores into games. My friend Lynda, a fellow homeschooling mom with four children and a hobby farm, creates games with incentives to work fast. "Who can pick up twenty things first" works well (fifty if there are guests coming over!). Another one is "beat the timer." Set the clock and see if you can clean up the living room faster than you did yesterday. If you're excited, the kids will likely be excited, too.

Chores and Gender

Be sure that you are not using the chore system to entrench gender stereotypes in your family. When I was a teenager, one of my friends used to complain that she had to do tons of housework, but her brothers got off scot-free. If you require your daughters to do more, or different, work than your sons, you may be perpetuating the role conflicts you're trying to overcome in your own marriage.

As the number of traditional households with stay-at-home mothers steadily declines, it becomes more unlikely that your sons will find wives willing to stay home and do all the housework. It is equally unlikely that your daughters will want to assume that role. In a large Canadian study of teenage attitudes, 95 percent of young women stated they planned to have careers—the same number as young men. And 85 to 90 percent also want to marry, have children, and continue their careers.[3] Some of these women may change their minds when they have to make agonizing decisions about child care, but most probably will not. You are thus doing your sons, and their future marriage partners, a disservice if you don't raise them to see household labor as the responsibility of the whole family. Try rotating jobs among your children regardless of gender.

Positive Feedback

Some women swear by offering incentives to their husbands, but I find this degrading and rather worrisome. We don't want to be manipulative; we want to be a team. And the usual incentive women use is, of course, sexual favors. I remember in an episode of *WKRP in Cincinnati*, Herb recalled that his wife felt sex was a reward—"Better mow the grass, Herbie, or no num nums tonight!" Never use sex as a reward. That's insulting and makes it seem as if you don't even value sex yourself. Instead, just be nice and say thank you.

Michele Weiner Davis, a psychologist who believes most relationship problems can be solved by all parties just acting smarter, says we can reinforce positive behavior by figuring out how we encouraged it in the first place. Identify the times when your husband and kids helped with the housework. Then determine what your role was in making it happen. Did you change the way you asked your husband? Were you more affectionate to him that morning? Did you spend more time playing with your children before asking them to help? Once you've figured out the pattern, repeat it.[4] Don't expect your family to automatically act perfectly since they have already done it once. Figure out how to change your behavior to continue encouraging their positive behavior.

Step 2: Instituting Consequences

The Purpose of Consequences

If you institute consequences when your family doesn't help, and you learn to stop over-functioning, your stress level may go down all on its own. Let's look again at the underwear-strewing husband. How can his wife change her behavior to encourage his participation in the cleaning-up process?

First of all, the problem is not really the underwear all over the floor; the problem is that she doesn't like having the underwear all over the floor. The placement of the underwear does not bother him. He could live every day of his life with the underwear there and his blood pressure wouldn't go up in the least. But she feels anger every time she sees the offending boxers. Maybe she has difficulty living in a room that is messy, or maybe she feels that he is being disrespectful to her. Whatever the reason, she is the one who feels tension about the situation, not him.

So how can she change? Ideally, she could take a psychological step back from the situation and decide just to leave the underwear there until he does something about it. I think this is unrealistic, since most of us would have a hard time constantly stepping over dirty underwear. Here's what I propose: she chooses a corner of the room or the closet where she can put everything he leaves on the floor. She should let him know what she's going to do, and make sure he knows she's not doing it because she is angry with him, but because she needs to do something to relieve her own frustration.

This way, she doesn't have to pick up after him, yet the room stays relatively tidy. Eventually he will run out of clean clothes and bring the dirty ones to the hamper. For her part, she needs to sort out her motives to be sure she isn't trying to start a fight. Remember that the purpose isn't to punish him but to help herself! Like Geri Scazzero said, it's not about getting someone else to do something. It's simply about putting limits around what you are going to do.

I should note here, too, that she shouldn't institute these consequences because of the offense itself (the underwear) but because of how she feels about it. My husband often leaves clothes around the bedroom (as do I), and every morning I just sort them all out. I don't feel he's being disrespectful—he's not like that in the bigger picture, and besides, he's not doing anything I don't do myself. But for this woman, the underwear was part of a larger pattern of disrespect, and she felt she needed to do something about it. What may seem horrible to one woman may not be a big deal to another. The issue is how things fit into the broader context of a relationship, and not each offense itself.

If it's just a little thing, please let it go! Your marital oneness is far more important than keeping track of every infraction. But sometimes that oneness is threatened because you feel taken for granted. In that case, don't punish him. Just set new boundaries yourself. You don't need to nag. You don't need to become angry. You just need to stop overfunctioning. And that may change things all on its own.

Geri Scazzero calls these small decisions of instituting consequences "unleashing the earthquake." You've decided to stop overfunctioning, as you should. And that's going to upset the balance and cause an earthquake in your relationship.

Every relationship is at some sort of equilibrium. We've all adopted our roles and responsibilities, and we know what to expect. That equilibrium isn't necessarily healthy; quite often it's not, and one person overfunctions and the other family members underfunction. But it is at equilibrium. We're used to it. The only way to change a dynamic like that, and to encourage those who are underfunctioning to pick up some slack, is for you to stop overfunctioning. You have to make the decision to change first.

This isn't a selfish decision, either. On the contrary, Scazzero believes, "this moment offers the greatest possibility for everyone involved to cross the threshold into an accelerated season of emotional and spiritual maturing in Christ."[5] By stopping doing too much, you can actually help your family members look more like Jesus.

Choosing Consequences

When thinking of appropriate consequences, you need to keep four things in mind. First, the purpose of the consequence is not to punish anybody but to find a solution for your own feelings of frustration. The consequence should make the situation better for you. Then even if your family doesn't help, you will still feel better than you do now. If you decide on a consequence that all understand, there will be no more fighting or nagging, just acting. The whole process takes a lot less time, and you can use that emotional energy for more positive things. It's like Henry Cloud and John Townsend say in their book *Boundaries*: you're not setting boundaries on other people; you're setting boundaries on what you yourself will do.

Second, the consequence must never involve the withholding of love or acceptance. These are things we owe our family members simply because of who they are, and not because of what they do. It is remarkably easy, even natural, to decide that if your husband isn't helpful, you will become frosty, distant, or unaffectionate. Your feelings are hurt and you feel taken for granted, so naturally you may pull away. But this hurts everybody—your husband, who loses your love; your kids, who end up living in a tense environment; and you, who are also deprived of intimacy. This is precisely where appropriate consequences can help. Instead of withdrawing, do something that solves the problem and lets you concentrate on the relationship.

No matter how much we can damage our marriage by withholding affection, it is nothing compared with what can happen if we do the same for our children. Their identity is still being formed. If we teach them that they need to earn approval, we can make future relationships very difficult. No appropriate consequence involves emotional blackmail.

Third, family members must be free to choose the consequence without you getting angry. You aren't trying to control them; you're simply putting limits on what you will do. You will probably find, though, that if you are consistent, they will choose the consequence less and less.

Finally, the consequence must not be so extreme that you will be unable to follow through. If you back down and don't follow through after warning people about your course of action, you are teaching them that it is okay to disregard what you say and are further entrenching any disrespect they may feel toward you.

Consequences Help Children

God commands children to obey and honor you as their mother. Ideally this is a reciprocal relationship; you should make it easy for them to obey. This does not mean being lenient; on the contrary, it implies setting rules that they must obey, and teaching through consequences that obedience and respect are important. We should always gear the rules toward developmentally appropriate behavior, and we can't have so many rules that we exasperate our children. Yet if we do not set standards for behavior, we are denying our children one of the greatest blessings the Lord promises them (see Eph. 6:1–4).

As wonderful as King David was, he forgot this lesson. He was a very permissive father, failing to discipline his son Amnon even after grievous sins. This error eventually led to civil war (see 2 Sam. 13). By giving your children consequences and expecting certain behaviors of them, you are doing them a favor. You are teaching them to be self-sufficient, to be productive and responsible, to be considerate and helpful of others, to revere God and respect others, and to work hard. These are all important Christian virtues, but ones that all too many Christians lack because their parents failed to provide an environment where obedience and respect were actually required. If they are not taught to obey you, their earthly authority figures, how will they obey their heavenly Father?

Consequences Help Marriages

If your husband respects you, and feels that he is a great support to you, he will feel lucky to be married to you. But if you are doing everything for him, he may have a difficult time relating to you.

In Galatians 6:5, Paul admonishes us to "carry [our] own load." We need to be responsible for the things that naturally fall under our domain. He balances this by saying that we should "bear one another's burdens" in verse 2 (NRSV). The word for "burden," though, means something inordinately heavy. The "load," which we are to bear ourselves, refers to the natural conditions of day-to-day life. No one should be doing these things for another person, except as a gift of service. While such actions can be attempts to give such gifts—a commendable and lovely part of a working marriage—if done all the time, the line between servanthood and servitude is probably being crossed.

Think about it this way: if you had a maid, you would not expect to be her best friend. She is there to shield you from as much discomfort as possible and to do jobs that you don't like. On the British show *Downton Abbey*, for instance, Mary Crawley is fond of her maid Anna, but they're not kindred spirits. There's an emotional distance between them because they're from two different worlds. If you are acting like your husband's maid, how is he to have a relationship of mutuality with you? Certainly changing your communication and action patterns to fit better in a relationship of mutual respect may initially cause friction. If you maintain your perspectives of commitment and affirmation, though, you will probably work through it and emerge stronger for it. You will be forging a marriage where friendship more easily flourishes.

Again, the issue is not about what you do, but why you are doing it in the broader context of the relationship. There's nothing wrong with doing all of his laundry or doing the bulk of the housework. But if your relationship itself is one where you feel disregarded, and worry that you're not a team and that you don't have a relationship, then something needs to be done.

How do we choose consequences that will have these positive benefits for our relationships and make our lives easier? Below, I've given several examples of consequences that I think can effectively be put in place. These don't necessarily apply to all families. But for women who are wondering where to draw the line, these are good places to start.

Examples of Consequences
Don't Pick Up Things Off of the Floor
Rationale: Picking up toys, belongings, and clothes that family members leave lying around in common areas (not bedrooms if this is agreed upon) teaches them that others will step in when they are irresponsible.

Consequence: Create a "jubilee" basket, similar to the jubilee in the Old Testament, where all land is returned to its original owner after a set time. After children leave for school in the morning, or go out to play, you pick up everything left in common areas and leave it in a basket in the closet. You can return them on Sunday, or the owner can redeem them prior to that for ten or twenty-five cents, or whatever you think is appropriate. Believe me—if a child loses an iPod for six days, they'll think twice before leaving it lying around the house again.

On occasion, our family has had to do something more drastic. After repeatedly asking the kids to clean the playroom, or their bedroom, to no avail, we've hauled out the garbage bags and filled them with toys for the Salvation Army. If they had too many toys to keep tidy, then some had to go! Sometimes the kids helped us weed through, and sometimes they wailed on the sidelines as we confiscated stuffed animals they hadn't looked at twice in two years. But when there are fewer toys, it's much easier to clean up, and the kids aren't as likely to be overwhelmed by the task.

When husbands are untidy, pile their clothes and personal items in designated areas of the bedroom, and papers on a corner of a table or desk, so they can take care of them at their leisure.

Don't Do All the Laundry All the Time

Rationale: Laundry can be one of the most time-consuming, back-breaking jobs there is. It's also an essential life skill.

Consequence: Teach children how to do laundry and ironing at age-appropriate levels. Even eight- or nine-year-olds can learn to put in a load of laundry, as long as a stool is placed by the washing machine. And folding is a great activity to do in front of the TV (even for husbands). When children are old enough, give them their own hampers to do the laundry themselves. As writer Sue Careless says, one of the ways you know you're overworking is if you're still doing laundry for high school children.[6] For husbands, reduce ironing time by buying only wrinkle-resistant pants and shirts. And if you restrict your own wardrobe to knits, with few cotton or silk items, you'll have a lot less ironing to do all around!

If You Made the Dinner, You Don't Clean Up

Rationale: Food preparation and cleanup are also crucial life skills for all to learn. If you do all the cooking and all the cleaning up, a good chunk of your evening is used, though evening may be the only time you are together as a family.

Consequence: Once children reach the age of about seven or eight they can be taught to clear the table and do the dishes, especially if you have a dishwasher. Husbands can also certainly do this.

If this doesn't work, or your children are too young and your husband needs a break at night, you can institute low-maintenance dinners a few times a week until they do decide to help. Serve dinner with few dishes and no pots. Have cereal, or soup and cold cuts, or sandwiches, nuts, and raw vegetables. All the basic food groups are represented, yet it's quick to prepare and quick to clean up. You can explain to your family that you feel it is too much of a burden to always cook and clean up an elaborate meal, and so, until such time as they help, you are only going to make hot meals sporadically. Deal with the almost certain resistance by making good use of your freed-up time. Pull out the Monopoly game or the Old Maid deck and use this time wisely. Above all, reject the impulse to say, "If you would just clean up, we could have a real dinner!" Remember, the purpose is to spend more time together and have more fun. If you are perfectly happy eating Corn Flakes at 6 PM, they may sense the impending minimalist fare and start helping soon!

When children grow older, have them make dinner once a week. Ten or eleven is a good age to start this. A ten-year-old can boil spaghetti and heat canned pasta sauce. Then you clean up. If you tell the child that he or she can plan the menu for that night, it gives them added incentive to help you. This can be an exceptional service to your child. One prominent chef in Toronto offers a cooking class to high school students where they can learn how to make healthy, tasty meals, like stir-fry or lasagna. When they finish their first year away at college, they invariably return singing the chef's praises because their house has become one of the most popular spots on campus! Being able to cook a good meal is a very useful and attractive skill, and it can be fun to teach kids. They're also more willing to move out when they're nineteen or twenty if they know they won't be consigned to a future of takeout and frozen dinners! They feel self-sufficient.

But kids aren't the only ones who can help with meals. If you work outside the home, having your husband be responsible for a few meals a week may be invaluable to you. Using the methods for effective communication, ask him to fix dinner once a week, as a start. Then, don't complain if it's simple, burnt, or even takeout. As long as you don't have to cook, and it's nutritious, who cares! Ideally, you could all be rotating nights once children are in high school.

Dinner Should Be a Time for Family Discussions and Socializing

Rationale: Children need to have a time when the whole family is together and can talk for an extended period without outside distractions. Studies regularly show that one of the best predictors of a child's healthy emotional life, his or her high academic performance, and other benefits is eating together regularly as a family. If mealtimes are haphazard, or everyone eats and leaves too quickly, you are losing one of the precious times a family still has together. Family reading, devotions, and prayer flow naturally after dinner, but if family members scatter, a valuable opportunity is lost.

Consequence: If they will not sit at the table, you can deny them other privileges, including whatever it is they are rushing to get to. You could make a rule that there is no telephone or television until later so that conversing as a family becomes more attractive. Turn the Wi-Fi off in the house from 5–7 to encourage family time. If husbands don't agree, you can still enforce the rules with the children. In far too many families, even holiday dinners that have taken hours to prepare are devoured in less than five minutes by family members who then leave the table for the cook to clean up. Don't let your family grow up like this! If your husband won't stay, encourage your children to anyway. They need as much time with the family as possible.

Children Must Respect Your Privacy/Personal Space

Rationale: Children need to learn boundaries with their parents. If they know there are certain ways you will always be separate from them, then they feel free to mature separately from you. If they have few boundaries themselves and/or don't respect yours, you are at risk of becoming emotionally enmeshed with them. Examples of reasonable boundaries are: they do not talk to you while you are on the phone; they do not yell at you through the bathroom door (or even worse, barge in); they do not bother you when you are napping or sleeping in; and they knock before entering your bedroom. Obviously these must be developmentally appropriate, but many children can start learning these things at two and a half.

Consequence: To devise consequences for these behaviors, first remember that children do things to get rewards. If you scold them for barging in on you in the bathroom but then give them whatever they wanted anyway, they are likely to barge in again. I suggest removing the reward for these behaviors. Or ignore them until a more appropriate time.

When children interrupt phone calls or other conversations, don't respond until you are free and they ask appropriately. You may have to explain to your caller why you are ignoring a screaming child. If necessary, hang up and discipline the child. He or she must learn that you are serious, or an important phone call will come one day and you will not be able to talk.

Respect for sleep time is another thing many parents pray for. When children are old enough, they can be taught to let you sleep on weekend mornings. You can facilitate this by anticipating what they may need and making it accessible. When my cousins were young, my aunt put plastic bowls, spoons, and cereal on the bottom shelf of the kitchen cupboard, and the milk in the bottom of the fridge. To this day, her bowls are kept down low, though my cousins have both now graduated from university. You can also put favorite DVDs by the TV and lay out crayons and paper for them. Hopefully, this will buy you an hour or two!

Don't Always Rescue Your Children When They Forget Something

Rationale: Children must learn to be responsible for their own schedules. They should show you respect by asking for help ahead of time if they need it. If you jump in when they forget their lunches, or drive them to school when they miss the bus, they will learn that someone will always cover for their mistakes.

Consequences: Let's look at some rescues and come up with some appropriate consequences. If your child forgets his or her lunch habitually and is always calling home to have you bring it to him, try not doing it. Your child will not starve after one hungry afternoon. It may be a good idea to inform the teacher or the principal of what you are doing and why, so that they do not assume the worst of you!

If your child is notoriously late, choose an activity that is not crucial to you to make your point. Tell her she has to be ready by a certain time and you will give her no further warnings. If she isn't ready, that's it. You don't go. You may have to do this a few times, but she will learn to be on time.

When my cousin was three years old and attending a preschool, my aunt had a horrible time getting her ready in the morning. So one morning when Shawna wouldn't get dressed, my aunt simply took her to school in her pajamas with her clothes in her bag. The teacher took one look at her and said, "Oh, Shawna, we don't come to school in our pajamas." The other children echoed her, and Shawna never did it again. All fights for her to hurry up were over.

All Family Members Must Call or Text if They Are Going to Be Late

Rationale: Courtesy requires that people respect each other's feelings. We all worry if someone is late, and everyone has an obligation to prevent that. Plans often revolve around who is going to be home at what time, so courtesy demands that schedules be communicated.

Consequences: If children do not call when they are going to be late, deny them the privilege to go out. If they are late from soccer practice, then they should miss the next one. If they are late after a social engagement, they cannot go out the next night. Some husbands often have the terrible habit of staying late at work or with friends, leaving you wondering whether to eat dinner without them or to wait. Usually, you get frustrated, the kids get hungry (and whiny!), and dinner is unpleasant for everyone. If this is a frequent problem at your home, I suggest having a set time for dinner. After dinner the food is put away and all latecomers must fend for themselves. If you make dinner twice or even three times each night, saving it and reheating it, you are teaching your family that consideration does not matter and are losing the irreplaceable opportunity for low-stress family dinners.

If your husband or child phones and tells you he or she is going to be late, by all means save or delay dinner. But if it becomes a habit, consider before you make dinner twice.

Practicing Servanthood with Consequences

While these consequences may be appropriate to teach respect and responsibility, servanthood also calls for flexibility. Perhaps your teenage daughter is frazzled studying for her SATs or because her boyfriend just broke up with her. It may be a good time to exercise grace and do her chores for her, giving her a consoling hug and some time off. There is always room for exceptions when children need it, or simply because you want to give them a gift of help or time. But if you do not exercise consequences on a consistent basis, they will become ineffective, and you will have few options left to encourage your family to take responsibility for household tasks.

Getting Outside Help

Finally, if you have tried everything and help is not forthcoming, here are a few other ideas to lessen your load:

Share Housework with a Friend. See if you can take a friend's children once a week while she does a big clean, and then you can swap. Or better still, go in with a third woman, and see if you can get two of you to clean a house together. This works wonderfully for spring cleaning!

Make Meals with Other Families. Arrange to have a meal bank with another family. Each of you prepares enough dinner for two families. The leftovers are stored in an agreed upon freezer. Whenever you make a deposit, you can also make a withdrawal. This works with as little as two families, but you get more variety with more people participating.

Hire a Maid. If you can afford it, hire a housekeeper. Many women seem reluctant to do this because they think it means they are not doing their job, or because it's a waste of money. But how much is your time and peace of mind worth? If you can have someone come in and clean for a few hours a week, freeing you up for something else, why not do it?

Quick Reality Check

What consequences can you put in place for your husband and children that can lessen your own frustration level? Pray about these first to make sure your motivation is to increase your family's harmony and respect, and not to punish them.

For Deeper Thought

1. Do you make it easy for your children to obey you? Are your rules understood, firm, and consistent? Are you comfortable with the idea that they should obey you, or does that seem harsh? Read Hebrews 12 and get a picture of how God disciplines His children. Ask Him to help you do the same for yours.

2. Does your husband respect you? Does he value what you do? Should you make changes in the way you relate to him so that he can more easily respect you?

3. Meditate on the difference between Galatians 6:2 and Galatians 6:5. Are you carrying your family's burdens, but making sure they carry their own loads?

Chapter 8

Kids Spell Love T-I-M-E

*M*y oldest daughter left for university this year. Her younger sister is trying to cope with major Rebecca-withdrawal, and I'm trying to adjust to not knowing everything that's going on in Rebecca's life. She's doing wonderfully, but it's still a hard transition for those of us left behind.

At university Becca has an active social life. She's involved in several campus Christian groups, and she's on several worship teams along with her studies. Not surprisingly, then, her evenings are quite full. During the day, however, if she doesn't have class, she often wants to connect. So she'll phone. In the middle of the day. While I'm trying to get work done.

I miss my oldest child very much, and I pray for her constantly. Yet too often, when she's on the phone, I start thinking about everything I need to get done. I wonder how long she wants to talk, and how soon I can get back to my important stuff.

Then I give myself a big shake, shut my computer down, and listen with rapt attention, because I want to stay connected. And if it means that I move some of my work to the evenings, when she's less likely to talk, then that's what I'll do.

Kids are not convenient. They're not convenient when they're eighteen months, and they're no more convenient when they're eighteen. One of the first things you learn as a parent is that your time is not your own anymore. Kids rarely do things on your schedule; they have their own timetables and their own ideas. And if you want to build a great relationship with them, so that they do want to share things with you when they're eighteen, you need to stop thinking of your to-do list and start thinking of the precious child who is in front of you, trying to get your attention.

The Parent-Child Chasm

Growing apart from your kids is not usually intentional. Few people consciously decide, "I'm not going to spend any time with my children." Yet we all know people who don't seem to have any relationship with their kids at all. Poor relationships are only natural in our antifamily society. They're the default setting. Connecting with kids today means going against the grain. It means breaking through social media, video games, and extracurricular schedules. It's not easy, and it's certainly not natural. It's easier to go about your daily routine while your kids scatter, only to return to eat or grunt something monosyllabic when you ask about their day.

The good news is that because such a chasm is usually unintentional, with effort it can be crossed. And that effort is worth it. The family has proved to be the best—and some may argue the only—place for children to learn morals, values, responsibility, and commitment. Increasingly, though, children are not getting the time they need with parents to have these lessons passed on. Judith Harris, in her book *The Nurture Assumption*, claimed that parents have become irrelevant to their children. Her study showed that by the time kids reach their middle years, peers, teachers, and the media hold far more sway over their opinions, dreams, and values than their parents do. She believes this is improving societal solidarity. I think this should be our call to action. We know our kids need us, so how do we buck society and meet these needs ourselves?

Bridging the Gap

Over 3,500 years ago, God gave us the answer. In Deuteronomy 6:5–7, He says:

Love the Lord your God with all your heart and with all your soul and with all your strength. These commandments that I give you today are to be upon your hearts. Impress them on your children. Talk about them when you sit at home and when you walk along the road, when you lie down and when you get up.

Our primary role as parents is to teach our kids about Him. Yet how we communicate these truths may be almost as important as communicating them in the first place. God didn't tell us to take our kids to Sunday school once a week so they could hear someone else talk about Him. He instructed us to spend time talking to them throughout the day, when they get up, and when they go to bed. Why did God do it this way? I think it's because when we invest time in our kids they feel loved and valued. They see we care, and so are more likely to respect us, listen to us, and emulate us.

Instinctively we know this. That's why magazines are filled with articles on how to maximize quality time with your kids. Yet God doesn't tell us to condense our time with our kids into short, meaningful bursts. He wants us to spend time with them, period. The idea of quality time doesn't appear in the Bible, and I think for good reason. Talk show host Dr. Laura Schlessinger, a big proponent of the family, says, "Quality moments require quantity time to occur spontaneously."[1] You can't just make them happen.

Certainly you can schedule your playtime, say for Tuesday after school. Maybe you can all play Battleship together. It's important to devote exclusive time to having fun with our kids. These activities build goodwill, trust, and affection, and provide a place where kids share their hopes and fears. But these activities shouldn't be the sum total of your relationship. They're what's necessary first, to move toward the end goal. Kids need to see that you value them enough to spend time with them; then they'll feel free to connect.

But if we're relying solely on planned playtime to connect emotionally with our children, our plans may backfire. Imagine that on that particular Tuesday your eight-year-old daughter's best friend told her that she was only her third best friend, or your ten-year-old just found out he didn't make the soccer team. They may not particularly feel like being with you at all, and the time you planned to spend communicating has suddenly evaporated.

Often the best times of communication we have with our children aren't planned. They're the lazy afternoons when we sit around making cookies and your son tells you that he's been having problems at school because no one wants to sit with him at lunch. Or maybe he's thinking about quitting karate, but he's worried about what you'll think. When you're spending time with your children on a regular basis, this kind of communication happens naturally.

When You're Not a Barbie/Tonka Trucks Mom

All this talk of quantity time may scare you silly, though, because you look at your day stretching out before you and wonder, "What on earth will we fill that time with?" How will you entertain the kids?

I totally get it, because I absolutely hated "playing" with my girls. I'm not one of those sit-on-the-floor-and-play-Barbies moms. Even the idea made me want to run screaming in the other direction. Yet what if there's another way to look at quantity time—a way that looks a lot more like the Deuteronomy mom than it does a mom who can pull off a Barbie wedding or a Tonka Monster Truck rally? Deuteronomy doesn't tell us we have to play with our kids all the time. It simply says we have to interact with them, and the best way I always found was to involve my girls in my life.

In fact, I always found it easier to involve the kids in my life than I did to try to enter theirs. When I was cleaning the kitchen, for example, I'd give them a cloth and a spray bottle of water and they'd go to it with the bottom kitchen cabinets. We'd talk and laugh and they would be "helping Mommy."

We also folded laundry well together. While I was folding, I'd throw sheets up in the air for them to run under, like a balloon. And then, when they were done with that, they always got to fold the pillowcases and the facecloths into nice squares.

Even though they were entering into my sphere, they were "playing." They were laughing and having fun. And they felt as if they had my attention because I was laughing with them and talking with them. I figured I had to clean anyway, so if I could involve them, then I was playing and doing my own chores at the same time. Then later on, they might let me have some downtime!

Sometimes I think we demand too much of ourselves, thinking that good parenting involves climbing into the sandbox. There's nothing wrong with that, but that may not be who you are. But if you involve them where you can, where it's more natural for you, as often as you can, then they won't feel abandoned if you make them play by themselves at times.

Children feel secure when parents pay attention, laugh with them, and try to teach them things about the world. They learn, "I am important. I am loved. The world is an understandable place, where someone will always help me to figure it out. And my Mommy thinks that I can handle it."

Isn't that what we want?

Too many parents, though, find the idea of interacting with their kids a little daunting. They have no idea where to even start. I have a vivid memory of sitting in a doctor's office across from a mother with a toddler. The little boy was squirming and swinging his legs. The mom would ignore him, but every now and then she would swat his legs and hiss, "Eric, sit still!" He became dejected, and wiggled all the more, because he was bored.

If we think of outings and errands not as things we have to drag kids to, but as opportunities to teach them and to talk with them, perhaps we wouldn't feel so exhausted or dejected ourselves.

Let me illustrate this with one of most people's least favorite activities with kids: grocery shopping. My two daughters and I never had much of a problem shopping together, because I had strategies (I was also only juggling two children, not four or five as some of you are, admittedly!). Here's what we did at the different ages:

1. Babies
I kept up a constant running commentary. "Mommy's buying broccoli. See the broccoli? Yummy!" Up and down the aisles, I'd talk and maintain eye contact as much as possible, despite the strange looks I'd get from other shoppers!

2. Older babies, toddlers

Upon entering the grocery store, I'd head immediately to the produce aisle and buy bananas or dried fruit snacks, one for each child. After grabbing these necessities I'd pay at the express line and keep the receipt handy so I wouldn't be challenged later. Now the kids had something to eat while we shopped.

Then we'd launch into the color game. "Let's see how many things we buy that are yellow! What's yellow? Butter's yellow! Lemons are yellow! The wrapping on the spaghetti is yellow!"

3. Preschoolers, kindergarteners

We graduated to letters. How many things can we buy that begin with the letter "B"? Bread! Butter! Broccoli! The girls would scan the shelves for things that started with the B sound, even if we weren't buying it. If I picked up popcorn kernels, I'd say, "Does this begin with B?" And then they'd debate and try to figure it out, because P and B are awfully close.

And then all the way home, they'd scan signs for the letter B. The next time we'd move on to D, or P, or M.

4. Elementary schoolers

Now we had two games! We'd play the "food group" game, where the girls had to name the food group. And if there wasn't an obvious food group, it was likely processed food, which meant we shouldn't buy it.

Then we brought math into the picture. How much do you think this is going to cost? We'd round everything to the nearest dollar and they'd try to keep a running tally, and we'd see how close we got. As they grew older, we tried rounding it to 50 cents.

I'd also start sending them for some things themselves (but always together). I'd say, "Can you two go get the milk?" or "Can you two go get the chocolate chips?" (They never minded the latter request!)

5. Teenagers

You're never too old for a game in the grocery store. Today we play: who can guess closest to the total cost? The winner gets to choose what we have for dinner.

We Stress Discipline Too Much

My girls and I loved watching episodes of *Supernanny* together, and one of the things that we've noticed is that so many of the dysfunctional parents don't actually talk to their children. They may carry their children around all day, but they don't say anything to them. And if their kids start whining or talking, the first response is to stick some food in their mouths, or try to deflect them with a snack.

Children are naturally curious. Their job, as children, is to learn how the world works. Our job is to help them. And yet sometimes I don't think we parents give room for our children's natural curiosity. If you can channel it into something healthy, then they're far less likely to start screaming in Wal-Mart. And the neat thing is that the more you interact with them (even if it's just while you're on errands), the more they'll play quietly without you for at least a few minutes at a time because they know Mommy loves them. They've already been talking to Mommy for hours.

This is a crucial lesson for many parents to learn, because too often we do parenting backwards. Most parenting books focus on discipline: what to do when the child starts to act up. Yet if you interact with your kids, talk to them, and show them that they are important, they are far less likely to do anything that requires discipline in the first place. Besides, too often we confuse children being bored out of their minds with children being disobedient. To discipline a child because they're whiny due to boredom isn't fair. How much better to pay attention to that child and help them feel valued instead!

You Are Enough for Your Child

Talking with your kids, pointing out interesting things when you're on errands, and teaching them things sounds a lot like a buzzword we hear in education circles today: stimulation. Children need stimulation, we're told, or they won't do well in school! But we often think stimulation is something that is best done by those with training, not by "just" moms.

When Rebecca, my oldest, hit three, I was wracked with guilt because I wasn't "stimulating" her enough. Many of my friends had enrolled their kids in expensive preschools, where they played at story centers, and sand centers, and paint centers. All Rebecca had was me! Sure we went to the library, and went swimming at the Y, and went to playgroup, but how could I make up for this lack of professional stimulation?

Luckily, I got over it, and Rebecca fared perfectly well. But I don't think my experience is unique. One of my friends, after leaving her job to become a stay-at-home mom, continued to send her older child to the sitter every afternoon because she was afraid he wouldn't like being home with just her. Instead of feeling guilty for putting kids in care, we often feel guilty for not putting them there. Yet studies repeatedly show that being home is as good—if not better—than any alternatives.[2] And this doesn't end when kids go to school. My friend Lynda embraced an opportunity to retire early so she could be home when her teenage daughters arrive home from school. Lynda feels they need her now even more than when they were young because of all the tough issues they're facing. So she hangs out with her daughters, and their friends now hang out with her! They have a wonderful relationship, and her girls appreciate Lynda's support and advice.

Take heart! You can do the job! You are the only mother your kids have, and deep inside, whether they act like it or not, your kids want time with you. Maybe you think your sister, or your friend, or your neighbor is a better mother. But they are not your child's mother, you are! So hold your head up high and jump in!

Limiting Outside Obligations

Part of embracing this role of mother is learning that the family should be the center of the child's life. This used to be normal; today it's not. When I was a child, children tended to be involved in one outside activity, whether it was gymnastics, a sports team, or music lessons. The new trend is for a child to try a little bit of everything. It's quite easy for him to be involved in three or more things each week. Add several children to the mix, and the schedule quickly becomes overwhelming.

While we may want every opportunity for our children, it's important to keep the big picture in mind. Perhaps there are ways they can participate in something without it being a weekly event. When my children were younger, they loved gymnastics, so we decided that would be our weekly lesson. But they also wanted to take swimming and dance. During the summer, we sent them to one-week day camps for each of these things. That enabled them to get a taste of both without ruining our schedules throughout the year.

Kids need time just to be kids: to play together, to relax, to develop new imaginary worlds, and to conquer new lands (even if these consist of pillows on a floor). They need time to play with siblings, something that can be difficult if they're always going their separate ways. Don't be afraid to say no to another activity. Teens, too, can become easily overwhelmed with opportunities for extracurricular activities, youth group, and part-time work. You may need to limit the number of nights they can be out each week. They are at risk for burnout and losing all touch with you at a point in their lives when they need guidance the most.

Sometimes the tables will turn and it will be you who has to turn down an opportunity. Maybe you won't serve on that committee because it meets Wednesdays and Wednesday is one of the few nights when your family is actually home together. The more you prioritize home life, the more opportunity you'll have to bond with your kids.

Limiting Outside Intrusions

Limiting outside obligations may succeed in keeping your children corralled in your house, but it may not necessarily give you more time with them. Too many things inside our houses compete for their attention. Imagine that as soon as your child arrives home, a stranger arrives on your doorstep and announces that he wants to spend the next four hours telling your child rude stories and jokes. He also wants to make sure your child sits perfectly still, not getting any exercise. He wants to do all this in your child's room where siblings, friends, and especially parents won't bother him. What would you do? Most likely call the police, right?

And yet something not too different from this happens when we let our kids spend their lives on screens, whether it's TV or the Internet or video games. Most of us would admit that limiting screen time would be for the best, yet the thought of actually taking the plunge and limiting, or even eliminating, these things makes us queasy. According to a 2010 study reported in the *Journal of Pediatrics*, the average preschool child spends four hours in front of a screen.[3] And the average elementary age child spends seven hours in front of some sort of screen every day.[4]

While there's questionable content on TV, there can be downright dangerous content on the Internet. We want to let our kids use the computer because we want them to become technologically proficient, but let's face it, most of the time they're on the net, they're not hanging out at the Library of Congress website or researching homework. And social media is now the primary place that bullying occurs.

It's unlikely that you want to ban these things outright, even if you could do so without provoking World War III. But you can take steps to limit negative influences:

1. Relegate all television sets to an out-of-the-way place, such as a corner in the basement, to make them less attractive to watch.
2. Put computers in a central place, so kids will be less inclined to surf inappropriate sites. Install parental controls to protect your kids—and you—from temptation.
3. Get rid of your satellite dish and cable TV. Take the money that you save and use it to do something fun with your family, like monthly bowling, mini-golfing, or a pizza party.
4. Maintain access to all your children's social media accounts (if you decide to let them have them). Don't let them keep passwords secret.
5. Limit children's time on video games. Turn these into a treat rather than a constant habit.
6. Make a list of all the things your children like to do for fun, and place it somewhere prominent, like on the fridge. Then children can choose something to do when they're bored. Remember, when kids have to find something to do, they will.
7. Designate certain times as technology free, such as dinner times or family nights.
8. Turn off the Wi-Fi at a certain time each night—say 10:00—so

that the kids (and you and your husband!) won't stay up late surfing on phones or other devices.

And let's not forget that our kids are not the only ones with the problem! When I wrote the first edition of this book, the main problem people had with screens was TV. Today, just ten years later, I frequently see young moms taking kids for walks in strollers, while those moms text at the same time. Instead of our children getting our undivided attention when we're out, we're spending it on our devices. Leave the phone in your pocket and talk to your children!

Increasing Family Fun

While having rules to minimize time stealers is a good idea, an even better idea is to give your family fun activities to fill their time. Make family dinners a priority. Dinnertime is often one of the few times when families can be together and talk about what's going on in their lives. Too many families lose out on this sharing because of outside commitments, or, in 40 percent of cases, because TV drowns out any potential conversation.[5] Some families also carve out time by planning weekly or biweekly family nights. Our pastor and his wife often gather their four children together for a Friday video night, when they can lay back and have some fun together. You can be sure that on those nights the kids aren't begging to watch TV in their rooms or trying to make phone calls to friends. As kids get older, if you let them choose what to do on family nights, they're more likely to participate, and they'll appreciate you for trying to connect.

Dads and Kids

Finding that quality time, talking to our kids, and limiting screen times can do wonders for helping us feel more connected to our children. Despite our best efforts, though, there is no substitute for an active father's role in the life of the children. Nothing that a mother can do can actually make up for the father. David Popenoe, a sociology professor at Rutgers University and codirector of the National Marriage Project, says, "What fathers do—their special parenting style—is not only highly complementary to what mothers do, but is by all indications important in its own right for optimum child rearing."[6]

In a nutshell, mothers and fathers interact differently with children. Fathers, he says, emphasize play, while mothers emphasize caregiving. And when fathers play with their kids, they tend to be doers, helping build bridges with Legos, or acting out specific scenarios with action figures. They encourage kids to focus on the task at hand. Mothers pick up a doll and say, "Who is this? What is she doing today?" They allow the kids to be in charge. When the kids respond, moms follow along. Moms nurture imagination.

Popenoe also asserts that parents adopt different parenting roles, together making a good parent but separately being inadequate. One parent frequently meets most of the child's need to feel nurtured and loved. Often this is the mother, though this is not always the case. However, this same parent may also tend to be overprotective. The other parent, on the other hand, is the one who most encourages the child to become self-sufficient, and learn healthy competition and life skills. He (or she) doesn't fulfill the nurturing role as well. Every child needs the complete picture.

When He Needs Your Prayers

The first action you need to take to encourage your husband to be with your kids is to pray. In Malachi 4:6, the very last verse of the Old Testament, God promises that John the Baptist will come to turn back the "hearts of the fathers to their children." And the angel speaking to Zechariah about John's birth in Luke 1:17 promised this same thing as the first order of business. Claim this promise in your prayers for your husband.

When He Doesn't Have Enough Time

Let's look at what we can do about some of the common roadblocks to your husband spending time with your children. In many houses the problem is not that the husband doesn't want to be with his kids, it's that he doesn't have the time because of his job. In some families, his job may also leave him in no mood to play when he does get home. After battling commuter traffic to work, spending a long day there, and battling the same traffic home, he just wants to collapse.

Obviously this situation can be frustrating for a wife. Just remember he's probably frustrated, too. He sees himself as working hard for the family, and if he senses your resentment, he may retreat even further. Men thrive on appreciation, so try to look at things from their point of view. Be appreciative for what he does do. Don't diminish the importance of earning money, but thank him for his effort. Just let him know that the most important thing to you isn't how much money he earns but the relationship you all have together as a family. If you can talk about his schedule in a non-blaming manner, making it clear that you love him, you may be able to problem-solve to find more time.

If that's not possible, though, you can try to make the time he does have with the kids meaningful. Some families organize "date nights with Dad," where the fathers take out each child individually for a special time of bonding. Or he could perform one ritual, such as always reading to the children before bed. Don't dictate to him what he should do, but brainstorm ideas with him so he can find some he feels comfortable with and excited about. His efforts to connect with the children will go a long way to grow the relationship, even if hours and hours of attention aren't possible.

When He Can't Relate to the Kids

But perhaps the main problem isn't that Dad doesn't have enough time; it's that he doesn't seem interested. Until recently, men haven't been conditioned to think that their primary job is to care for the kids, so it's not necessarily as easy for a man to bond with his children as it is for a woman. But take heart; this is often only a temporary problem.

When a baby is born, there's plenty for a mother to do. She nurses whenever the baby's hungry; she's the one the baby summons in the middle of the night. Many an eager father has been hurt by the apparent "rejection" of a baby. He can't console the child, despite his best efforts, whereas his wife picks up the baby and instantly the wailing stops.

But when that same child reaches three or four, and is able to play rougher games, the real bonding with Dad often begins. There's also a period of bonding just after the birth of a second child. Mother is needed for the new baby, and another pair of hands is needed for the older child. Dad suddenly finds himself indispensable, and falls into fatherhood more naturally, even if a little late. So before you start making an issue of your husband's lack of involvement with your kids, look at your family situation. Is this something that may change once your child reaches another stage? If so, keep praying, and keep the long-term picture in mind.

When He Needs You to Step Aside

In some cases, though, there's something more drastic we need to do: take a huge step backward. I think we women often work against our husband's bonding with the kids for one simple reason: we expect dads to act like moms. When I first took Rebecca home from the hospital, I spent hours hugging her against me, loving the feeling of this tiny person snuggled close. My husband, on the other hand, would hold her at arm's length as he vigorously bounced her up and down. I, of course, was petrified. Had he not been a pediatrician, I probably would have demanded that he give my baby back. But he insisted she liked it, and Rebecca did seem to stop crying. I just tried not to watch.

The first time Rebecca laughed was when her dad was doing something that looked dangerous, so she obviously was not scarred for life from this treatment. But Keith's reaction to Rebecca is often quite similar to other men's; they try to play with the baby, rather than comfort the baby. And we women, feeling protective, often stop them.

This doesn't end once the infants become toddlers. We often have very definite ideas of how men should care for the children, and because we're afraid they won't do it properly, we don't always give them the freedom to try.

I remember one story a friend of mine told of a summer she and her husband spent with another couple at a cottage. One day the women decided to take a day off and go shopping, leaving the men with the five kids. The men looked at each other, unsure what to do, and then yelled, "Hey, who wants to go to the beach?" Naturally every child started jumping up and down enthusiastically, so the dads grabbed five bathing suits and jumped in the van for the twenty-minute ride.

Upon arriving there, they realized one bathing suit was too small, so this child swam in her underwear. They had brought no pails and shovels, no snacks, and no drinks. One dad went to buy some chips and pop, while the other collected seashells. The kids rolled in the sand for sunscreen, having more fun than they'd had in ages. On arriving home, though, the mothers had apoplexy because their husbands had forgotten so many things. But they looked at their kids, who were grinning from ear to ear, and relented.

Sometimes men don't remember all the little things women do for their children, but the amazing thing is that they seem to make do anyway. That's often part of the charm of being with Dad—the way you have to deal with unforeseen circumstances. But if we don't trust our husbands with our children because we're afraid of such things happening, then we're depriving our husbands of a chance to bond with the kids.

Another reason we may not leave the kids with Dad is that this often constitutes more work on our part. When we have the kids, we let them play in the Exersaucer while we mop the kitchen floor, or let them play in the playpen while we cook dinner. Yet when men take over, they may forget these extras, and when we get home we have twice as much work to do. It just doesn't seem worth it.

Giving up is not the answer. When we were new moms, we probably weren't that good at juggling everything, either. It's something we learned. Men can learn, too, if we talk to them about what needs to be done and give them space to find their own ways of accomplishing everything. Yet even if men never do anything more than look after kids, this alone may be worth it because the kids spend time with Dad. The more they bond, the better for your kids, even if the extra laundry piles up.

When He Just Won't Spend Time with the Kids

What do you do with a husband who just won't look after the children, or worse, who is constantly going out with friends and leaving you alone? Talk it out. If you need more time alone, ask if he can take the children on a regular basis, such as one night every other week, so you can get a break. If you're doing the same for him, it's likely to work. But for many women, it isn't time alone they want; it's time as a family.

Make Being Home Fun

The best way to encourage family time is to make being home fun for your husband. Don't recriminate, nag, or insult him when he's home, but arrange to do something fun, like all play Monopoly, or have a special dessert. If you're enforcing discipline and requiring the children to clean up after themselves, the house will be even more inviting for him.

Encourage the Children to Share His Interests

We want our husbands to take an interest in everything our kids do. We want them to watch the kids' first soccer games or ballet recitals. But if your husband's just not interested in that, see if you can encourage your children to share his interests instead. Maybe he can take your kids to work with him occasionally. My friend Derek often took his school-aged sons with him to watch him fix trucks. They would play with their toy trucks while they were near Dad. Derek worked long hours, and if he had had to wait to be with the kids until he was home, he would never have been able to spend any time with them. When my own girls were younger, they would often go with Daddy to his office to play with toys there, or just to draw pictures while he was dictating charts. They weren't playing with Daddy, but they were playing near Daddy. They were with him and could see where he works.

Is your husband interested in computers? Maybe your elementary age kids can talk to him about that. Does he like fishing? Encourage him to take the kids. You can even try to include kids in the mundane things. If he's popping out to the hardware store, ask if he'll take a kid or two along. Maybe this just never occurred to him. The more he's with the kids, in whatever capacity, the better their relationship will be.

Don't Forsake Family Activities

Most men will take interest in their children if they're able to do it on their own terms. But if you're in the unfortunate situation where your husband just won't interact with your kids, no matter how easy you make it, here are some final thoughts.

Don't wait for your husband to take spiritual leadership in teaching your kids about God. Make sure that you enforce the house rules and introduce your kids to God, even if you believe these are tasks that should be assumed by your husband. Your kids need spiritual teaching, and waiting for your husband, even if you think this is an act of faith, could do them irreparable harm. Leave room so your husband can easily become part of the process, but do not neglect it.

Similarly, make sure your kids have fun memories of you and their siblings. Often we wait for our husbands before we plan big things as families. My friend Rachel was so busy waiting for her husband to do things with her and her son that she just sat around all day and did nothing herself.

Sometimes my husband is on call on weekends, which means going in to the hospital in the mornings and doing rounds, then seeing patients throughout the day. Probably about half the time, though, he's free by noon. Often on the weekends I wait for him to come home so we can all do something together. Because I assume he's going to be there, I don't make plans.

Nothing is more frustrating than when he doesn't make it home, and I don't have a clue what to do. The Saturdays that I decide to do something fun with the kids anyway, even if we miss out on seeing him when he's finished rounds, are usually immensely more satisfying for everyone. Much of life is like this. If your husband is always running to the office to do extra work, promising to return early but rarely doing so, maybe it's time to make sure you and your kids have a memorable time anyway, instead of waiting at home and growing resentful.

You may worry that this gives your husband permission to work all weekend, and to lose out on any potential time he may have with the kids. Valuing your children and giving them good memories is worth it. Nothing makes a child feel more rejected than waiting for their dad, only to have him not show up.

My friend Wanda was a pro at making memories for her children. The winter when she was pregnant with her fifth child, she hired a babysitter to share the driving and piled all the kids in the car. They drove to Florida (at least two days from our home in Ontario) to stay with relatives for a week. I can't imagine driving two hours without my husband, but she did it because she wanted the kids to have a fun vacation. John, who owned his own business, just couldn't take time off at that time of year, much as he would have liked to. So they had a great week, John worked extra hard while they were gone, and the kids had good memories. If Wanda were to have stayed home until John was free, such trips would have been far more rare.

If you lose your husband to work, friends, sports, or hobbies, don't lose your family, too. Make sure the kids are having fun, and you may soon find that your husband is making time to join you. Once you're not waiting at home for him—which many men interpret as an implicit guilt trip—but are active and having fun, he's more likely to want to be with you.

Floyd McClung, the founder of Youth with a Mission, writes in his autobiography *Living on the Devil's Doorstep* about an epiphany he once had.[7] He had been so engaged in mission work that he no longer knew his children. Then one day, in despair, he realized that his wife and his kids were the only ones that God had given him specifically to nurture. The lost, with whom he was so consumed, God had given to the church collectively. He did not give up his missionary work; he just changed his focus, and in so doing was more effective in every venue. Your husband and kids are yours specifically. When we prioritize them, and foster close relationships, we will feel more at peace and less frazzled because we're honoring our most important calling.

Quick Reality Check

1. Do you enjoy a close relationship with your children? If not, what are the main impediments? Is it time, lack of interest on either part, outside influences? What can you do to fix some of these impediments?

2. How would you characterize your husband's relationship with your kids? If it's not optimal, what steps can you take to help?

For Deeper Thought

1. Who are your children's biggest influences? You, the children's friends, church friends, the media? Do you feel like your kids hold good values and are following Christ, or are they being pulled away?

2. What do you enjoy doing with the kids? When are you most relaxed with them? Ask them to choose two things they want you to do with them, and decide to do these this week (even if it's playing Barbies or crash-'em-up cars on the floor).

3. Look at your schedule and see if your kids, or even you, are involved in too many things. What can you cut out to give you more time as a family?

Chapter 9

Bringing Your Wallet
Under God's Control

*H*ave you ever noticed that the way we define ourselves usually centers around issues of money? "I'm a homemaker" means I work at home rather than earning income elsewhere. "He's an accountant" gives people an idea of the salary he commands. But this emphasis on financial identity is relatively new. In times gone by, we would have introduced ourselves as "John Smith's granddaughter" or "Janet Smith from Philadelphia." Money is now the central defining feature of our identities, so it's hardly surprising, then, that money tensions often rear their ugly heads in our families.

Popular culture is full of images of this financial tug-of-war between husbands and wives. Do you remember the episodes of I Love Lucy, when Lucy would overspend and Ricky would discover her transgression and bellow, "LUUUU-CY! What did you do with my money?" A decade later on The Flintstones, Wilma and Betty smiled conspiratorially and raised their hands in a battle cry as they yelled, "CHARGE IT!" The money disputes portrayed in shows like these typically focused on her being too cavalier with his money. He earned it; she spent too much of it.

Many families still have attitudes similar to those of Ricky and Lucy. In other families, he spends too much on leisure; in still others she is considered inferior for not making any money herself. There's no end to the problems money can cause in a marriage. Jesus certainly said more about money than He did about heaven, or hell, or a myriad of other subjects. Our attitude toward money, it seems, often dictates our attitudes toward everything else. That's why "the love of money is a root of all kinds of evil" (1 Tim. 6:10). Part of the process of building godly families, then, has to involve sorting out our attitude toward money.

What Does Money Mean to You?

Money itself is not evil, and there's nothing wrong with having some or needing to earn some. But our attitudes toward it can cause problems. Too often people look to possessions and power to give them feedback about how they're measuring up. When we put our trust in something other than God, we're opening ourselves up for fights, jealousy, and all kinds of problems in our families.

Before we can even ask the big questions like "Should I work?" or "How should we spend our money?" we have to decide what money really means to us. In Acts 17, the Bereans took everything that Paul said and measured it according to Scripture to see if it was true. We need to be just as diligent with our attitude about money. Bible teacher Kay Arthur says that the biggest battle in the Christian life is with our minds, and the most powerful weapon we have in this battle is the truth we find in Scripture.[1] Here are some of the truths about money that you can use to measure your own attitudes:

1. Everything we have comes from God (James 1:17).
2. Our most important possessions are heavenly ones, not earthly ones (Matt. 6:19–21).
3. We must be financially responsible. We should make sure we do not depend on others (outside the family) for our livelihood. "If a man will not work, he shall not eat" (2 Thess. 3:10).
4. We should be content no matter our circumstances. Paul says, "But if we have food and clothing, we will be content with that" (1 Tim. 6:8).
5. Our identity is based on what Christ did for us and not on anything else (Gal. 2:20).
6. We are to be generous and give to those in need (1 Tim. 6:18).

Even with these guidelines, though, different families will come to different conclusions about how much money they need. Janet Luhr, in her book *The Simple Living Guide*, recounts the story of a family with two children who lived on a small sailboat. Their cost of living was so low that they could afford to work sporadically, spending most of their time together instead.[2] Other families may choose to live in a small apartment, while still others feel they need to own a house in the suburbs. There's nothing inherently wrong with any of these choices, as long as the families bring their desires before Christ.

God calls all of us to different things in life, so we will all make different decisions. Indeed, these decisions about money and work are often gut-wrenching precisely because God allows such freedom. Let's look at some common areas of financial decision making, and see how we can make decisions that glorify God.

Should I Work?

Most of us today grow up with the expectation that we would work—certainly until children came along, if not after as well. We trained for it; we planned for it; we dreamt of it. And work certainly does have plenty of benefits. In many families, the wife's income allows the family to own their own home or to send their kids to Christian school. It provides them with a certain security. If something ever happens so that the husband can't work, she can still pay the bills. It gives women a social network, intellectual stimulation, and a feeling of accomplishment. And it provides women with an opportunity to use the gifts God has given them in the wider world.

Most of my friends work, and I understand why. I always assumed I would work, too, but that changed the day I held my daughter for the first time. I think many women want to stay home, but the things work offers pull them away. In fact, an astounding 84 percent of working women told *Forbes* magazine that staying home with the kids was something they aspired to.[3] Many women who work fulltime feel conflicted. I think such torture can be solved by examining the reasons for working.

Of course, this process itself seems unfair because people rarely ask men, "Do you think it's right for you to work?" Yet it often is phrased like this for women, because women are thought to be the caregivers for children. Personally, I don't think it matters greatly which parent is home with the kids. In some families, the ideal would be if both could work part-time—and get paid handsomely for it! Nevertheless, women are more likely to want to stay at home than men are, and so we are often the ones who wrestle with this question.

Who Should Care for the Children?

When we're trying to make this decision, as with everything else, the main motivation should be what is best for the family. This is the antithesis to what we usually hear: that we have to do what's best for ourselves because only then will we be happy and able to care for our families. Yet Paul says, "Each of you should look not only to your own interests, but also to the interests of others" (Phil. 2:4). He's saying that our needs are certainly not inconsequential, but at the same time they are not paramount. Those who are likely to be most affected by your working are the kids, so it's important to look at their needs, too.

Should someone stay home with the kids, or is it okay to leave them in day care? And once the kids are in school, can you manage a close family life if the wife works? Too often we don't allow ourselves to even ask these questions. We assume work is inevitable since we need the money. Try to put financial considerations aside for a minute and look at what the kids need. About work, Dr. Laura Schlessinger asks us, if we were to be born again tomorrow, would we choose to spend our days in a day care or in the care of a parent? Few of us would choose a day care, she says, so why would we choose it for our children?

Of course, most of us who leave kids with others don't choose a day care where no one knows our child personally. Only 23 percent of all preschoolers with working parents are actually cared for in such centers.[4] Most kids whose parents work are cared for by relatives, like grandparents and aunts. Other tots are sent to neighborhood homes where the care is given by people you know personally, though the quality of such care can vary quite substantially. Nonetheless, all these kids are missing out on time with their parents.

Many studies exist showing conflicting findings about the possible effects of day care on children. But one of the best studies shows that children who are left in day care for twenty hours or more a week are more likely to be violent, and 55 percent more likely to be insecurely attached to their mothers—no matter what the quality of care provided.[5] Jay Belsky, one of the leading researchers in attachment and day care, said this after conducting a large-scale study:

> Children in any variety of child care arrangements, including center care, family day care, and nanny care, for [20 or more hours per week beginning in] the first year of life, are at elevated risk of being classified as insecure in their attachments to their mothers at 12 or 18 months of age and of being more disobedient and aggressive when they are from 3 to 8 years of age.[6]

The problem doesn't end once children go to school. Mary Eberstadt, in an article titled "Home-Alone America," writes about the detrimental effects from millions of kids being left at home alone after school. She says this: "The connection between empty homes on today's scale and childhood problems on today's scale cannot possibly be dismissed as a coincidence."[7]

When we make decisions about work and child care, we must do so with children in mind. Some will choose to work because it's financially necessary. For others, it means financial sacrifice to stay at home or to work part-time. But this is not a life sentence. There is always time to pursue a career later. Life doesn't have to be lived all at once; it can be lived in chapters. My friend Bonnie, a family physician, chose not to work for three years while her husband completed his residency in emergency medicine. Some may say she was wasting all her training by staying at home, but she didn't think so. This was her season to be with her kids, and now that they're in school, she's returned to work half-time.

I don't mean to suggest that everyone who chooses to work fulltime is choosing wrongly or putting their children last. I know most women find themselves completely torn up and make such decisions only very reluctantly. But even if you're putting your children first, you may still be at a loss about whether or not to work, because children are not the only considerations. Let's look first at the financial considerations and then turn to other factors.

How Much Money Is Enough?

When Tim and Nicole's third and last child was nine months old, Nicole decided to go back to work. She felt they needed the money for all the extras they wanted for the kids, so she took a low-wage job in the mailroom of a newspaper. She earned $10 an hour and paid her sister $3 an hour to babysit her two youngest. She also had to pay for a second car, snacks, take-out meals, and work clothes. Then, of course, taxes took a huge bite. I would be surprised if she took home more than $2,000 a year after all these deductions were sorted out.

Whether working is financially necessary has as much to do with the cost of working as it does the salary you can expect to bring home.[8] In some families, that $2,000 can be all that's keeping them from losing their house. In such a case, the decision to work is quite different than in families where the $2,000 is what's standing between them and the latest Playstation. It's important to get an accurate picture of earnings before you commit to a lifestyle that is bound to be hectic.

If you're confused about these financial considerations, the chart on page 165 can help you sort this out. Total up all the possible monthly costs of working, including child care, extra clothes, transportation, cellular phone charges, dry cleaning, and food eaten out because you don't have time to make dinner. Next, figure out how much you would earn in a month and look at the difference.

The fictional woman in the sample chart on page 165 works in a union secretarial position at a local school for $17 an hour. It's not a bad salary, and she's happy to get back to work. She puts her two-year-old in full-time care with a lady down the street for $25 a day, and her five-year-old in care half-time when he's not in kindergarten. The family decided that with her job they needed a second car and bought a used one on credit. She needs to look presentable at work but has gained some weight since the kids were born, so she needs to buy a few outfits this year. She also finds herself spending more on cosmetics and haircuts than she did before.

Item	Sample Amount	Actual Amount
Child care	$750/month ($500 for one child full time; $250 for another for half days during kindergarten	
Transportation	$200 car payment $70 insurance $100 gas $50 maintenance	
Coffee/Snacks bought out	$2/day x 20 days = $40	
Lunches bought out	$5/day x 6 times a month =$30	
Work clothes	5 outfits a year, or $40/month	
Dry cleaning	$10/month	
Buying takeout for dinner	$20 x 5/month = $100	
Cosmetics	$20/month	
Other		
Total Expenses	**$1,410 /month**	
Salary	$17/hour @ 35 hours/ week = $2,578/month	
Taxes, union dues, and other deductions	$620/month	
Net Salary	**= $1,958/month**	
Net Take-Home Pay	**= $548/month**	

The family finds that they don't seem to have a whole lot more money at the end of the month, even though she's returned to her $30,000-a-year job. After you do the math, the reason is obvious. Once you take all her expenses into account, she's actually only taking home about $548 a month. To put this in even cruder terms, instead of making $17 an hour she's actually making $3.61. Is it worth it for her to work if all she's making is $3.61 an hour? What about you? What is your time worth? Or, to look at it another way, how much money do you need to fulfill your family's goals?

My friend Barb is frantically trying to answer these questions. She has four children, ages seven to twelve, and now that they are in school full time she would like to supplement the family's income. Even a little more money would ease some of the financial pressure on the family. The problem is that she already feels pulled in all directions. She's not sure what kind of a mother she would be if she were even more exhausted and frenzied. She's trying to decide how much she needs to work, and if she can find a job that fits into a reasonable schedule. Before you take a job, do what Barb is doing and thoroughly investigate all the possibilities. Make sure the job contributes to your family's economic stability significantly enough to warrant working.

The good news is that families can come up with all kinds of creative answers that can still maximize their time with their children. In some families, the wife works while the husband stays home because she has a higher income. Other families creatively manage their work schedules so that the husband and wife work opposite one another, and one is always home. (The danger, of course, is that the spouses never see each other!) Still other families make use of very generous grandparents or other relatives to reduce the cost of child care. Some women work only part time, enough to keep their professional credentials and earn some money while still being home the majority of the time. And some start home-based businesses, or become consultants for one of the many direct-sale businesses, like Tupperware or Mary Kay. Several women in my church represent these organizations. Though they could earn more money with a full-time job, they choose to earn less, and work less, because it meets their needs.

Then there's the opposite approach embodied by Amy Dacyczyn, author of *The Tightwad Gazette* books, whose claim to fame is not that she makes so much money but that she saves so much money. A penny saved is a penny earned! If by staying at home you can find ways to save your family money, either by creatively grocery shopping and cooking, searching for bargains, or doing much of the family work yourself rather than buying ready-made products, then it can be as if you have a job. Once you've done the math and looked into the possibilities, you'll have an idea about whether you financially need to work. Now let's look at the other considerations.

Who Are You?

For many women, money is not the primary issue in making decisions about working. My mother, who is a career consultant, recently met with Cathy, a professional, poised woman in her early fifties who had been offered an attractive retirement package due to company restructuring. Though her colleagues were falling all over themselves to claim this windfall, she was reluctant to take it. At home she was treated as a nobody. She was expected to make all the meals, do all the vacuuming, do the laundry, and clean up after her teenage son. At work she was respected. Her opinion was sought, her advice heeded, and she felt important. She couldn't bear to lose that respect.

Many women can identify with Cathy. They went to school for years, and now they spend their days talking baby talk, mashing up bananas, and doing endless loads of laundry. Nobody cares about their brains anymore! If you were to look at them with their messy hair, no makeup, and little bits of baby food stuck all over their sweatpants, you would never guess these same women could function very well in a professional setting.

Even though I completed two master's degrees, earned numerous scholarships, and actually have more degrees than my doctor husband, everyone thinks of me as "Keith's wife." My friend Laurel and I often commiserate together about how we're looked down on for not having careers. We feel we're doing the most important job in the world, but it's just not acknowledged!

Part of the reason is that being home seems awfully mundane compared to being at work. The rewards from work can be tangible, immediate, and very attractive. This is not necessarily true from child care. The simple fact is that kids fight, vomit, cry, and make huge messes, and you get little respect for dealing with these problems. In many ways, it's easier to work than to stay home and entertain a two-year-old. My friend Kate confessed, "I just think staying home would drive me nuts." And Marjorie Williams, a columnist for the *Washington Post*, writes that she hopes one day her five-year-old will understand that, to her, "What I do at that desk feels as necessary to me as food or air."[9]

Why is staying home with kids viewed so negatively? Perhaps one reason is that it's isolating. While women may once have had friends and family nearby, we now find ourselves alone on our street. While mothers may once have sent the kids to the park to meet with other kids, we now find ourselves literally fenced in with our own backyard equipment.

Instead of enduring this, we choose to work. I find myself wondering if Marjorie Williams would feel work was "as necessary as air" if she could just find some way to replicate some of the benefits at home that she gets at work. For instance, if work gives you social contacts, you could join a gym, a playgroup, or a ladies' Bible study. If work gives you a sense of accomplishment, you could join a committee, organize a church or community fund-raiser, or pursue education online or at night school. And if work gives you intellectual stimulation, you could read the paper, learn a new skill, or start a letter-writing political campaign at home. Even money can be found at home—although maybe in smaller amounts—by operating a home-based business. If you want to stay home, but are afraid you can't handle it psychologically, investigate ways like this that can replace some of the benefits of work.

Do I Need to Do My Share?

In my final year of university studies for a master's degree in sociology, I met with my supervisor to discuss my future plans. This woman, a respected mentor of mine, had published extensively on the unpaid work that women do (namely housework) and the contributions this makes to the economy. When I told her that my husband and I had decided I would forgo the PhD because we wanted to have children, she was crestfallen. I had great intellectual potential, she felt, and I should not waste it by staying at home.

This was devastating to me, but in a funny way, solidified my resolve to stay at home. If this woman, who had devoted her life to championing stay-at-home women, still viewed these women as making poor choices, then I didn't want any part of academics. I thought the feminist agenda existed to give us a choice about whether we wanted to work or stay home, and then to extend these same choices to men. Instead, the movement tended to label any choice other than work as inferior.

This label has ramifications for how husbands and wives feel about their financial obligations. Instead of the money the husband earns becoming the "household money," in a pooled account in both of their names, many husbands and wives now keep separate bank accounts and are expected to both contribute to paying the family's expenses.

In the same way that the sexual revolution freed men from the obligation to commit to women by offering sex without marriage, the gender revolution has also freed many men from feeling an obligation to support the family.[10] After all, single women with children manage to work, so why can't my wife?

Bill, our mythical 1950s husband from chapter 2, would never have asked such a question. It was his role to provide for the family; that was the way he showed love to his wife. But Rick, our modern husband, wants Carissa to work to help support their lifestyle, and Carissa has accepted this reinterpretation of her role. Just as many women embraced the sexual revolution as freeing to their bodies, so women have embraced this revolution, claiming it frees their minds. They are able to reach their potential, to use all their gifts, and to do otherwise is a waste. Whatever the benefits of the gender revolution in the workplace, it has tremendous impacts on marriage relationships and expectations.[11]

When a man and woman marry, they become one person in every area, including their finances. The only judgments that are important regarding money, then, should be those that best help the family to glorify God. Many women, though, are uncomfortable with this situation. It could entail relying on their husbands to support the family.

It goes against the grain to be taken care of and requires a great deal of trust and humility. But the benefits can include putting your trust and identity in God, rather than in what you do.

Other couples struggle because he clings to the idea that she must earn her keep. Rather than taking into account the value of the work she does at home, the only thing that seems to matter is the size of her paycheck. My friend Rachel felt she needed to work because her husband was always pressuring her to bring in some money. Even though he made enough to support the family, she took a part-time job so that she could have some of her own cash. She was tired of feeling guilty for spending his money, a view he shared. Though this is a much stickier problem, it is often based on unspoken assumptions. If you feel strongly that you want to stay home, talk to your husband about the benefits of having a parent home with the kids. Explain your reasoning and work out a budget showing that it is financially possible. Hopefully as you talk through these issues, he'll begin to share your vision for the family too.

Your Habits

Our attitudes about money are one half of our family's financial picture; our actions are the other half. Here we'll look at how to bring our own spending habits under God's control, and how to adjust if our husbands don't share this vision.

Are Your Spending Habits Responsible?

My friend Diane, whom I mentioned earlier, bought expensive clothes for her children, frequently took them to McDonald's for lunch, and, in general, spent a ton of money on them—though admittedly she spent little on herself. Her husband, Ted, gave her money each week to spend on groceries and necessities, but it never seemed to be enough. So one day she applied for a credit card. She told Ted about it and said she would only use it for emergencies. Soon it was run up to its limit with clothes from Disney and Osh Kosh, and she was in trouble. After delaying as long as possible, she confessed all to Ted and a huge fight followed.

Ted may have been unfair to Diane in how much he allocated to her to run the household. But that does not excuse Diane from being unfair to him in return. Many times she would react in anger at not being given enough money for groceries by buying the children expensive outfits. She was "paying him back" for his stinginess by punishing him financially. In the end, they all suffered.

Other women don't overspend out of revenge; they spend simply because it's fun, because they want to compete with their friends, or because they're bored or lonely. When I'm in a funk, I have to admit that having a new outfit or some new cosmetics feels great. But if we splurge every time we're down, we could end up with closets overflowing with things we'll never wear and a credit card bill that will last well into our social security years!

Responsibility with money is crucial for family harmony. It lowers our own stress, reduces marital conflict, keeps us on track spiritually, and leaves a great example for our kids. I have developed a spending system that works well for us, gleaned from a variety of money management books. I admit I've never been able to stick to a budget, the kind that said you spend $42 on entertainment this month and $478 on groceries. It was too time consuming, restrictive, and picky for my personality. But I still wanted to make sure I was responsible. Keith and I sat down one day and figured out how much we had to spend on retirement savings, short-term savings (for a new car), mortgage, and utilities, as well as other nonnegotiable items. The remainder each month is allocated between us. I divide my portion into four, and that's how much money I get a week. If I want to spend it all on groceries I can; but if I want to scrimp on groceries one week and buy a nice outfit the next I can, too, without feeling guilty, because the essentials are already paid for.

Living with a Miser

When Esther and Robert were first married, they were the typical starving students. Esther worked to support her husband as he completed his PhD, but they had very little to spare. Robert thought that all frivolous spending should be weeded out, and to him that included the lipsticks Esther liked to buy from time to time to give

her a pick-me-up. At the same time, he felt it was perfectly justifi-
able to spend money on books, since he would need these for his
future career, however nebulously they related to his specialty. So while
Esther couldn't spend ninety-nine cents on a tube of lipstick, he could
spend ten times that on books.

The interesting thing about this, of course, is that it was Esther
earning the money, but she still felt like she had no say on how it would
be spent. Other families have the same results though the roles may
be reversed. Rachel used to bemoan the fact that her husband would
spend money on golf games while she wasn't allowed to do anything
fun herself. He worked all week and needed a break, he said. She had
a break all week.

What do you do if your husband is irresponsible with money, either
because he spends it lavishly or because he refuses to let you have any
for yourself? By this point in the book you're probably quite familiar
with my plea to let love reign in your marriage, love which keeps no
record of wrongs. Resenting him for his spending habits is unbiblical
and just builds up bitterness, which can kill affection. That being said,
you may still need to find a way to protect yourself and your children
if your husband is not leaving you enough money.

I am not a big fan of strict budgeting, since I could never stick to
one in the first place. But if you are having these sorts of problems,
a budget may be the answer. Many men, such as Robert, aren't concerned per se about frivolities but are worried about their financial situation. Instead of developing an actual budget, they may decide to live
by the creed "don't spend on anything stupid" (although the definition
of "stupid" is usually left to them!). By suggesting you budget, you let
your husband know that you are on the same page; that you, too, are
committed to keeping the family solvent, and that you, too, want to
be responsible. Most men will welcome such a move!

Figure out what your "nonnegotiable" spending is, such as the
bills you have to pay every month for cars, mortgage, insurance,
taxes, utilities, savings, and so on. Then, as long as you're meeting
your obligations every month, call the rest negotiable. Determine
how much you have left over and decide how to allocate it to both of
you. For instance, if you have $800 left, you can ask for the majority

if you are the one shopping for groceries, clothes, and household supplies. If you stick to your budget, and he sticks to his, you don't need to worry if he golfs, and he doesn't have to worry if you buy lipstick. You're both living within your means and being responsible, and you don't have to resent him for spending money that he doesn't let you also spend.

If, on the other hand, your problem is that he spends money indiscriminately, using credit, then you have a bigger problem. If your husband seems unwilling to dedicate money to ensuring the financial stability of the family, you may need to take it upon yourself. You can use some of the money you have each week for groceries and clothes, and put it aside, perhaps in a savings account or a money market account. Then, if you ever become overburdened with debt or need some money in a hurry, you have access to emergency funds.

Some families, though, require more drastic action. Spending habits, either yours or his, have left you with debt you can't deal with. Seek help before it gets worse. Many churches have Christian financial counselors who can help, and most towns have credit counselors. If you can manage to swallow your pride, they can help get your finances back on track—and lift a huge burden off you in the process.

Do You Know About Your Family's Financial Picture?

If your husband were to die in an accident today, could you locate his will? Do you know where your retirement savings statements are, where your bank statements are, or even how to pay the credit card bill? Do you know the difference between a stock, a bond, and a mutual fund? Do you know what you own? Do you know what you owe? Do you know your family's plan to ensure your financial stability?

If the answer to any of these questions is no, then you could have a serious problem. Many men take care of the household finances and enjoy this activity, feeling that in doing so, they are playing their role as provider. Nevertheless, it is important that you know how to do it, even if you don't do it yourself. Let's face it—it's easy to leave everything to him so you don't have to think about it. But that's definitely not responsible! You'll be safer in times of crisis if you know how to care for your family's finances. And if you understand the financial plan your husband is working with, you'll be able to participate more easily. Maybe you have some good ideas on how to save money, which you've never mentioned because you hadn't realized how little there is in the children's college savings plans. Being aware of your financial situation helps you partner with your husband and protects your financial stability.

Do You Give Money Back to God?

The final area of potential conflict revolves not around whether it's his money or her money, but how much is actually His. As a family, are you committed to returning money to God by giving some away? I have talked to wives who would like to be more generous with their money, but their husbands don't agree. They don't want to "waste" family money on charities.

I know that the Bible says to put tithing first, but if your husband does not hold these values, other verses take precedence. You need to protect your marriage, so don't go behind his back, even if it feels like the "righteous" thing to do. It's actually dishonest and sows conflict.

That does not necessarily preclude, however, you tithing the money that is in your hands. If you have decided on a certain amount of discretionary income for yourself, which covers the family expenses, you may want to consider giving some of that money away. Don't do it in secret. Show him that you can manage to do both, and he may not mind, and God will bless you for it. Still, I do not believe that God requires you to endanger your marriage over tithing. Your love and acceptance of your husband, along with, and especially with, your prayers, form the best route for opening him up to the grace that God showers upon those who are generous.

Money is a loaded issue, fraught with difficulties for nearly all married couples. Yet, like all problems, the answer lies in keeping our attitudes like that of Christ and acting in a responsible manner. If we look at money the way God does, decisions about work, values, and spending will be much easier. Money will lose its hold on us, allowing God to grab us tighter. And as we move closer to Him, the money problems standing between us are bound to diminish.

Quick Reality Check

What are your money attitudes? Are you fearful of the future? Do you crave more and more stuff? Do you feel unimportant if you're not working? List five main feelings you have about money. Are these godly? If not, ask God to change your heart.

For Deeper Thought

1. If you struggle with financial worries of any kind, try to meditate on what the Bible says about money. Use the verses provided in this chapter and spend particular time on 1 Timothy 6 and Matthew 6, which talk about how to develop good attitudes about money.

2. Are you being responsible with your money? Take a "mini-snapshot" of your spending habits by keeping track of how you spend your money this week. Are there areas you could improve?

3. If you work outside the home, what benefits do you get only from the workplace? If you want to stay at home but are scared of losing these benefits, in what other ways could you meet these needs outside of work?

Chapter 10

In the Mood

It's 10 PM. The baby's finally settled. You've just finished cleaning up the kitchen, which looked like it had been hit by a hurricane rather than just by three children under the age of six. Dirty pans from two nights ago still sit soaking in the sink, but you can't find the energy to tackle them. One more night won't hurt.

You drag yourself up the stairs glancing at toys strewn across the living room. No evidence remains that the kids actually tidied up earlier. Sighing, you change into your flannel pajamas, take one last peek at the children, and decide to collapse into bed.

But before your head hits the pillow, your husband, who has spent more time tonight finishing up paperwork than actually talking to you, intercepts you. You know the look on his face. He's not interested in affection. He's interested in action. You let him kiss you for a few minutes before pushing him away. "I love you, honey, but I'm just really tired, okay?" You hope to avoid the big fight that often follows when he accuses you of never being interested in him. You don't want someone else on your back after you've dealt with people whining and clinging to you all day. You just want to sleep.

Throughout this book I've been looking at how to help us feel less exhausted and more like a family unit, even if your husband isn't as invested in the process. But in this chapter I'd like to turn the tables a bit and ask you honestly, "Are you doing everything you can to make your marriage better?" And to most men, sex is a huge part of that equation.

Many of us can point to mountains of things that our husbands don't do: they don't play with the kids; they don't pick up their underwear; they don't put the dishes in the dishwasher. They never even talk to us! These things very well may be true. But if you decide that because you feel distant and because you feel tired then he can't expect sex, then you're jeopardizing your marriage, too, and you're hurting yourself in the process.

Of course it's difficult to maintain a healthy sexual relationship when your lives feel so hectic. But when marital intimacy is lost, everyone suffers. You don't feel like a unit; you feel like two warring factions with competing interests where one must always lose. The kids sense the tension and wonder at its cause. They'll either worry reflexively that they're at fault, or think emotional distance is normal in a marriage.

If one of the reasons that you're distant in the bedroom is because the kids are eating up so much of your time and energy, then you need a big reality check. I know this sounds harsh, but please hear me: once you're parents, your marriage matters more, not less, because now other people are counting on you to get this marriage thing right. Your kids need your marriage to be rock solid and stable. And sex is a huge part of that.

Change Your Attitude Toward Intimacy

It sounds like a generalization, but I have yet to talk to a couple who does not deal with this tension: she makes love because she feels loved, and he makes love to feel loved. In other words, when she doesn't feel loved, the last thing she wants is to make love. But when he feels distant, the thing he wants most is to make love because that's how he fixes everything. Seems like a recipe for disaster, doesn't it?

If your husband is not treating you with respect or helping you run the house, it's awfully hard to feel romantic when the lights go down. You're tired. You're overworked. He doesn't appreciate you. He doesn't help with the kids. You get so little time off. You just want to be by yourself!

You're probably perfectly justified. Most women deal with these tensions. He has no right to expect you to make love when he doesn't help you around the house or attempt to woo you. But here's where I'm going to get controversial—so what? So you're right. Being right doesn't help you to be happy or to form a close marriage. Does being right relax the tension in your house? Does it rejuvenate your soul?

As hard as it is to do, I want to challenge you: let go of your need to be right and just love him. This is the better strategy for several reasons: it's exercising the love we're commanded to show; it reduces tension; and it is almost guaranteed to make your marriage better. And when the marriage is better, he feels more goodwill toward you and is more likely to help you with the things that frustrate you in the first place. It's much easier to talk problems out with a husband who appreciates you than one who feels bitter.

I have no illusion that this will be easy. And if you're having a specific disagreement, you probably need to resolve this first before intimacy is possible. But if it's just a chronic malaise, and if you can find the fortitude to rise above it and get back "in the mood," you'll likely find yourself solving some of the problems that were bothering you in the first place. He'll feel more generosity toward you, and your outlook on the marriage will likely improve.

Stop Bitterness Cold

Bitterness squeezes out any affectionate feeling you may have, so it has to be purged if you're going to revive your relationship. I know this can be tough, but think of it this way: When are you happiest? Probably when you feel close with your husband, right? Is your bitterness standing in the way of this? Then it's time to let go of it. Some of us have much larger doses than others. Some of us may not be bitter at our husbands at all, but just bitter about the course our lives are taking because we have so little time to devote to what we want to do. But whatever the cause of the bitterness, we have to let it go.

In the same chapter of the Bible where God tells us to lay aside every weight, He also says this, "See to it that no one misses the grace of God and that no bitter root grows up to cause trouble" (Heb. 12:15). Bitterness causes trouble in our marriages. It makes us miss out on the grace of God. When we're bitter, we harbor our own self-righteousness and carry with us the sins of others. How can grace reach us if we're so sure we don't need it? Instead, God reminds us that the meek will inherit the earth. God lifts up those who concentrate not on others' faults but, in humility, see their own.

Some have almost overwhelming burdens of bitterness, perhaps caused by infidelity. Letting go will be difficult and will probably require some help. And reviving intimacy may not always be possible—or even advisable—right away. But as much as possible, if we can root out bitterness, we will enhance our ability to connect in every way.

Stop Complaining

How many times have you been in this situation: you're sitting with a group of friends, and one of them recounts a hilarious anecdote about a time when she went away and her husband had to dress the kids. You can all imagine what a mess he made of that. He let their daughter out of the house with tights and a long shirt, but no pants! Or he put her dress on backward because he thought the buttons always go in the back!

The conversation then proceeds with everyone telling their worst husband stories and complaining about how men don't understand what women go through. I've been in plenty of conversations where, I'm sorry to say, the focus has been on how men fail when it comes to being able to look after basic domestic duties.

Often these conversations are in jest and aren't meant as true expressions of discontent. But here's the problem: you think about what you talk about. And if you're always talking about your husband's inadequacies, you'll start to look for things that he does to confirm this impression. Instead of noticing that he was especially sweet with your son tonight, you'll latch on to the fact that he didn't clear his dishes at dinnertime. And if you engage in these kinds of conversations too much, you're encouraging other women to endanger their marriages as well.

Recently I read that Catherine Marshall, a woman of deep faith, felt convicted by God about being too critical. In response, she decided to stop cold turkey from saying anything judgmental. She was amazed at how little she actually talked that first day. She would begin to make a comment and then felt compelled to stop. But then a funny thing happened. When she stopped being critical, she noticed the nice things people did. She started writing encouragement cards. Her mood was lighter![1]

Let's lay aside our criticisms, even those made in jest, because they can be one of the heaviest weights holding us back as we run our race.

Stop Talking with Toxic People

If someone is toxic to you, avoid him or her. Solomon said, "Stay away from a foolish man, for you will not find knowledge on his lips" (Prov. 14:7). All of us know toxic people who leave us feeling angry, depressed, or envious every time we encounter them. If being around someone turns your thoughts to negative things, it's time to reconsider how much time you spend with that person.

If you have a friend who is always complaining about her husband, or who is constantly making jibes at yours, perhaps it's time to reevaluate that friendship. My friend Susan had a mother like that. Susan's mother, Monica, never accepted Susan's choice in a mate. To Monica, Geoff could never measure up. She told Susan this repeatedly before she and Geoff were married, and then visited their house frequently to note all the things that Geoff should be doing to make the house livable for Susan. When their children were born, Susan's mother phoned constantly to ask how Geoff was helping them. She would say things like, "Susan, you sound so tired. There's no way you can handle those kids with Geoff being so insensitive. You better leave them with me overnight. You need a break." Day in and day out she told Susan that Geoff should change or their marriage would fall apart.

Monica was toxic to everyone in that marriage. Not only did she drive a wedge between Susan and Geoff, she also made Susan question whether she could even handle the children by herself. Not surprisingly, Susan ended up leaving the marriage, claiming that Geoff just wasn't good enough for her.

Geoff was not what you would call an ideal husband. He did spend a lot of time socializing and very little time supporting or helping Susan. But instead of doing what she could to make her marriage better, Susan listened to a litany of criticism about her husband, which drove him further away.

It's hard to pull away from toxic people if those toxic people are your own parents or other members of your family. But you need to be free to work on your marriage by yourself without other people poisoning your mind toward your husband. There is one important exception: if he is abusing you, you may not be able to admit it to yourself and may need others to alert you. But other than in an abusive situation, it's best to eliminate influences that interfere in your relationship with your husband.

Decide to Love Him

Now that you've stopped the negative thoughts, it's time to encourage the positive ones. The principles of affirmation and commitment involve choosing to love your husband even if he stays just the way he is. Letting go of the dream of an ideal husband who brings home flowers and coaches baseball can be difficult. But if the dream is preventing you from seeing the good things he does, letting go of it is the best thing you can do for your marriage.

People who are married are healthier, happier, and wealthier than those who are not, and their children fare much better. One of the best investments you can make in your future well-being, and that of your children, is to build a better marriage. Keep your eyes open for things that you can respect and admire in him. Fifty years ago, a man would be appreciated for simply bringing home a paycheck. It was a big deal to be able to provide for his family. Today, that's considered almost inconsequential. It's difficult for men to live up to the many things that are expected of them. It's time to look at the things our husbands do and find things we can thank them for. Men react well to appreciation; they do not react well to judgment.

Recently my friends Derek and Lisa sold their car to us, with a local dealership acting as a middleman. In the process, the dealership made several grave errors that resulted in our being charged $1,000 more than we had originally agreed upon. This raised my blood pressure considerably. But I was thrilled when Derek and Keith both firmly told the dealership what they would and would not accept, and the dealership caved in. When discussing it later, Lisa and I both agreed that it was wonderful not to have to worry about these sorts of issues because our husbands were always there to defend the family.

Sometimes just little things like this are all we need to remind us how nice it is to be married. We appreciate the way they look after us financially, or fight to get the best deal, or go to bat for our kids when the school calls and says there are problems. Think about all the reasons you're glad there's a man around to do the things you like to avoid. If you tell him every time you notice something like this, he'll feel ten feet tall!

Writing down some of these insights can also prove useful later. Keep a gratitude journal where you list the things you're grateful for about your husband. Try to list one or two things he did today that you liked, even if they're really hard to find. If you concentrate on the positive things he did rather than the negative, your impression of him is bound to change.

Decide to Initiate

I think it must be very tiring being a man. I honestly don't understand this, but I know that every few days, men have a biological need to have sex. It doesn't matter what's going on around them—they feel it. And then they have to figure out how to get their wives to want it, too. Now, the last thing many of us want to do is initiate. Why would we try to make him even more interested in sex than he already is? Let me suggest a few reasons.

Sex Reaffirms Your Marriage

Sex is the only thing that separates your marriage relationship from all others. We have other relationships where we are loved unconditionally, like those with our parents and children. We can share our hopes and dreams with our friends and our struggles with counselors. We can live with roommates. But we can only make love with our husband. In the process, we reaffirm that we are married and committed to each other for life. If we let this aspect fall by the wayside, then we are saying there is nothing unique about this relationship. He could just be the buddy you talk to, the roommate you split rent with, or the father who provides for your family. And when this downgrading of your marriage occurs, the whole family is at risk. Both of you are more inclined to look to others to meet your needs—whether sexual or emotional. It's hard to provide a united front or spiritual leadership to your children when you're not united in other ways.

There may be instances, like illness, when sex isn't possible. In this case, the relationship won't necessarily suffer because of the emotional commitment you have made to each other. But when we routinely reject sex, oneness is threatened. That's why Paul warns that we aren't to stay apart for too long, and then only in mutually agreed upon situations (1 Cor. 7:5). He didn't say this because he expected women to simply acquiesce to their husband's every desire; he wanted us to preserve the marriage relationship, constantly reaffirming its uniqueness, preciousness, and exclusivity.

Sex Nourishes Your Relationship

If we don't come together intimately fairly regularly, the relationship will suffer. God designed sex as the way for a husband and wife to connect. And something spiritual happens when we do. That's why He says that the act of sex makes you one flesh, and why He warns against promiscuity. Few of us would disagree that when we connect sexually with our husband, we feel closer and happier than when we do not.

For some of us, though, this may not be true. Maybe you're having some sexual problems due to sin, physical problems, or what you feel are inappropriate demands. If this is the case, I recommend reading another of my books, *The Good Girl's Guide to Great Sex*, which helps you figure out how to connect physically, emotionally, and spiritually in the bedroom. It can be one of the most fun research projects you can take!

Whetting Your Appetite

Even if you've decided that you want to be intimate more often, how do you get yourself in the mood? It's not as easy for a woman as it is for a man, since we aren't programmed biologically to require sex so frequently and aren't aroused visually as much as we are emotionally. Can we change our emotions?

Absolutely, because our biggest sex organ is our brain. When our brain is engaged our body will follow. If you decide to concentrate on feeling sexy and intimate, and then set the scene for intimacy, you're more likely to desire it. Here are some ways to start this process.

Meet Some of Your Own Emotional Needs

Often the reason we don't want to make love is because we want something else instead—namely time alone. The evening, after the kids go to bed, may be the only time we have to ourselves. If we need that half hour before we crash to be alone, it's hard to want to make love! See if you can carve out other times during the day for your alone-time and other rejuvenation activities.

Make sure you're meeting some of your own emotional and intellectual needs throughout the day. Hire a babysitter for two hours so you can go out and do something fun for yourself. Or ask your husband to look after the children's bedtime routine so you get some time to soak in a bubble bath, read a novel, or just rest. Find ways to meet these needs outside of the only time you may have for intimacy.

Dream About Him

The lead up to intimacy can be just as sexy as the act itself—and if it is, the act is sure to be more meaningful for you. Try to get in the mood in the morning, long before he's even home. Put on lingerie under your typical mother clothes. Think of different scenarios where you'd like to romance him. (Make sure in these scenarios you're the one setting the scene. If you're dreaming of him initiating various things, and then he doesn't, you're sure to be disappointed.) Text him throughout the day. Make it a point to get through dinner and bedtime rituals quickly so you can be alone. Play mood music. Whisper sexy things in his ear and let him in on your secret. The more you let yourself dream and plan— rather than just waiting until 10:30 to see if you're in the mood—the more likely you will feel romantic when the time's right.

Whetting His Appetite

Setting the emotional scene is crucial because men don't want women who are willing to have sex; they want women who want to have sex. There's a huge difference. You may feel like you're acquiescing to him fairly frequently so that he has nothing to complain about. But if he feels you aren't putting your heart and soul into it, he may feel like something's missing—namely, the intimacy.

Other women may have the opposite problem. They're more than willing, but their husbands don't seem interested. They're more interested in work, or they're too busy, and seem to have lost interest in sex. A guy's decreased libido is often due to porn use, and if your husband seems to have little or no sex drive, it's worth investigating to see if this could be the root of the issue. If it is, deal with it by finding an accountability partner for him, installing controls on your computer, and even talking to a counselor together. You can't ignore it.

If porn isn't the issue, though, but you both just seem to have lost the spark that you once had, then maybe it's time to start a love affair with your husband.

When you were dating, did you take great pride in your appearance? Did you try to make yourself attractive to him, with attractive clothes and flattering hair? Most likely you did. Yet do you do these things today? Probably not. You don't need to attract him; you've already got him. And who's got the time? But let's face it—men react to visual stimulation. They like seeing us dress up for them. And how much do you feel like sex when you're wearing a flannel nightgown instead of a silk one? If you don't feel like you look sexy, you'll likely not feel sexy either.

My husband and I joke that if mystery is supposed to be the key to sexiness (i.e., someone wearing a slinky teddy is always sexier than someone naked, because there's something hidden), then my flannel "nightgown of mystery" must be the sexiest thing on earth because it leaves everything to the imagination. But of course, the opposite is true. A little mystery is a good thing; a lot is too much.

Another problem couples often face is that all the mystery is gone. When you were dating, he had to pursue you. Now you're there for him all the time. While a wonderfully intimate relationship can be forged when you spend all your time together, for many couples, it just doesn't work that way. If you are always there, available whenever your husband wants to talk and, in fact, pressuring him to talk, he's likely to feel crowded instead of cherished. You seem desperate to him, which is exactly the thing that would have made him run away when you were dating.

Don't let your life completely revolve around him. If you don't talk with anyone else, socialize with anyone else, or go anywhere without him, there is no mystery in the relationship. Instead of a lover, you become an obligation because you pressure him to be with you constantly. That's why you need to keep a life of your own. God made you uniquely you. It's okay to pursue your gifts, interests, or hobbies and expand your horizons. He does not have to be your whole life, and most likely he doesn't want to be. Meet some of your own needs yourself, so that when you are together, he can see you as an equal rather than one who is always making demands on him. This doesn't mean running off with friends all the time. But it may involve asking God where you should devote the time and energy He has given you, instead of waiting for your husband to fill the space.

Nurture Your Friendship

It may seem strange to talk about friendship after we've talked about sex. After all, shouldn't we feel like close friends before we make love? But I think in marriages, sexual intimacy often comes first. In many cases a husband needs sex to feel close to his wife. Then, once he feels close, he's more relaxed and more willing to explore other ways to boost the relationship. In the Song of Songs, the Shunnamite declares, after a deepening of their relationship, "my lover, this my friend" (5:16). The friend part, the more profound relationship, came later.

If you suggest finding ways to bond as a couple while simultaneously attempting to keep sexual intimacy to a minimum, then he may be unwilling and resentful, or feel like it's his obligation to do these things before you'll have sex. That's hardly a good foundation for friendship. Obviously we women would like friendship to come first. But if it comes second, we have a better chance of it growing!

It's easy to forget why you fell in love. Circumstances change. When you were dating, you had all the time in the world to focus on each other. Over the next ten years, you bought a house and a car, you started a career, you had children, and all of a sudden you have all these responsibilities and much less time for the romantic fun that used to characterize your times together.

Try to take some time again to date your husband. Arrange to spend some time alone together, at least every month. If you can't afford a babysitter, trade with friends so that they can have some time alone, too. You can even ship your kids to a friend's house, then have the house to yourself where you can have a candlelit dinner or just lie in front of the fireplace. Then, find things that you can do together. Some of these things you can do as a couple, but sometimes you may have to do them as a family. When kids enter the picture, it can be hard to identify fun things that you all enjoy. Try to find some new hobbies. Take the kids bowling or learn to rollerblade together. Go camping, or skiing, or tobogganing. Find things that you both enjoy that you can relax doing, even with the children. As you have more fun together, your relationship is bound to improve.

Practice Random Acts of Kindness

The last thing we can do to help breed intimacy is show our husbands kindness throughout the day for no reason at all. This shows him that no matter what, you accept him, love him, and appreciate him. Make sure that the ways you show him kindness speak his language. Picture this: you see your husband reading a newspaper while sitting in the recliner, and you walk over and start massaging his shoulders. He shakes you off and says, "Honey, I'm trying to read," and you walk away feeling rejected. But maybe you weren't speaking to him in a way he understands. Maybe your husband doesn't like neck massages, or it distracts him when he's trying to read. Don't do things for him that you would like done for you; do things that he appreciates.

Ask him what things he enjoys and keep track of what he reacts well to, and then do these things. By showing him acts of kindness throughout the day that are not contingent on his actions toward you, you show him that you care about him just the way he is. He is bound to feel closer to you.

Your marriage relationship holds everything together, yet it is easy to forget this vital relationship. We've talked about how to make your life fulfilling, how to make your house run smoothly, how to nurture your relationship with your kids, and how to prioritize so you feel less hectic and more focused. But for all of these things to have the most effect, you have to cherish your husband. It may mean stepping out of your comfort zone to seduce him or to make yourself vulnerable. But cherishing your marriage is the best investment you can make in your future and in the well-being of everyone precious to you.

Quick Reality Check

If sexual intimacy is a source of tension in your marriage, what steps can you take to make yourself feel more romantic? If this is difficult, pray that God will help you love your husband.

For Deeper Thought

1. Read 1 Corinthians 7. What is God's plan for a sexual relationship in marriage?

2. Think of some things you can do to nurture your friendship with your husband. How can you let him know you love being with him?

Conclusion

$\mathcal{W}$hen my husband and I recently drove through a beautiful rural area, I was struck by its rich history. Lining every meadow, for miles, were fences made out of stone. Not the pretty stone that we pay tooth and nail for from landscapers, but huge, backbreaking rocks, piled on top of each other. Each of those rocks had come from the fields. In order to begin farming, these pioneers of old didn't just have to clear trees, they had to haul rocks.

Our lives today are much more sanitized, but we still have those rocks to clear before we can begin to grow and bear fruit for God. And that takes a lot of work, a lot of sweat, and a lot of determination. The difference is that pioneers often had their eyes on goals that were much more straightforward. Today, we have endless chores and stress, and often don't know where we're headed.

I wish there were easy answers to the problems women face. I wish we could flick a switch and society would suddenly appreciate mothers and all the stresses in our marriages would disappear. I wish we could suddenly have, not more hours in the day, but less to do in the hours we have.

There is no magical switch. The strategies I've given you aren't plans you can implement overnight or panaceas that are guaranteed to solve all domestic problems. Instead, they are processes to help us figure out what is truly important, and then concentrate on how to prioritize these things in our families. And in these efforts, Jesus will be our guide.

Most of the problems start not because we set out to live in counterproductive ways, but because our whole society is counterproductive.

We value the wrong things. We emphasize money, self, power, and wealth. And even though we don't want to, we often let these mistaken priorities seep into our churches, our marriages, our families—even our dreams.

Changing our outlook to consciously think about what—and who—we're heading toward, and how we're going to get there, can help to pull up a lot of those rocks blocking us from growing. It will change us from the inside out.

My prayer is that as you make these changes, your families will change, too, and you can take the journey together. If they don't change with you, hopefully you will at least find a greater level of peace. If change does happen, imagine the army of strong Christian families we can unleash to demonstrate God's redemptive power. Take courage, take a deep breath, and plunge in. God longs to have families who value and respect each other, each blazing a new trail in this confused society. When we're part of His plans, we will finally understand what Jesus meant by the peace that passes all understanding (see Phil. 4:7).

Creating a Vision for Your Family

*A*re you familiar with the saying, "Without a vision the people perish"?

It's based on Proverbs 29:18, but I don't think God meant that just for the nation of Israel. I think He meant it for marriages and families, too. If we have no clear idea where we are going, then we will never, ever get there.

I have heard people say, "You can tell what someone values just by looking at how they spend their time," but I don't think that's necessarily true. If you look at many men, they spend more time on video games than they do talking to their kids. Does that mean they don't love their kids? And many women spend more time on Facebook every day than they do talking to their husbands. Does that mean they like Facebook more?

No, I honestly don't think it does. I simply think life happens. We love certain things, and we value certain things, but we're not intentional about actually living those things out. We don't take the time to figure out how to make those things part of our daily routine. And so, when other things threaten to crowd in, like technology, or screen time, or too many extracurricular activities, we let them. And then we wonder why we feel so unfulfilled, as if something is off, not quite right. It's because we're not valuing the things we should! It's because we're not living our lives with purpose.

We've been talking in this book about what to do when you feel like your life is out of balance; everyone takes you for granted, and things aren't quite right. I hope that the steps I've listed here have helped!

But if you want to take it a step further, I invite you to dream: to dream about what you want for your family, and what you want for your marriage, and what you want for your home.

If we don't take time to take stock, plan, and develop a vision for our family, it's very unlikely that we actually live out our values. Other things will creep in and steal our time.

And what is a vision?

A vision for your family, I believe, is simply a plan of how you will live out your values. God gives us specific visions about specific things we are to do. But sometimes I think we wait too much for God, and we don't bother to work with what He's already given us. And so I'd like to give you some tools to turn the values that you and your husband already share into a vision for your marriage and for your family.

Here's how it works . . .

I've included some worksheets here to work through with your husband. They're divided into three sections: character things (like what God wants to refine in you); the "feel" of your home (like what vibe you want your home and family to give off); and "calling" things (like what role God specifically has for you as a family).

I'd suggest working through this on three different "date nights," or nights when you set aside time to talk. Stress to your husband that this isn't about telling him what he is doing wrong; it's about you both thinking and praying about where your family is heading. His input is just as important as yours. I hope these bless you.

Part I: Character
How we want to reflect God

In Romans 8:29, Paul writes that we are "predestined to be conformed to the likeness of his Son." It is God's desire for us that we look more and more like Christ.

This will be the longest section in the visioning activity. There's a section for your own character traits, and a section that concentrates on your children's character traits and life skills. If you are parents, it may be good to do the "parent" part on a separate night.

Let's start by listing the three most important character traits that God is speaking to you about.

What THREE character traits do you think need to be manifested more in your life?

Examples might be: discipline, patience, joy, perseverance, hope, and/or trust.

Compare notes and pray together.

Pick ONE trait that you will each work on, and support each other in developing. (You can choose a different trait for each of you, or the same one that you will each pray about and work toward.)

Now break this down into something you will do. What new spiritual practice can I start to help develop this trait?

Examples might be: learning patience by taking time to pray when I get angry; learning to just meditate and think about God for ten minutes each day with no distractions; taking time together to talk with no screens.

Now what practical thing can you put in place to work on this trait?

Examples for patience might be: starting a 1,000-piece puzzle together; volunteering to help Alzheimer's patients; helping with the toddlers at church.

Brainstorm together: How can we live out this character trait together as a couple more?

Now let's turn to life skills. Looking more like Jesus isn't just about matters of the heart; Scripture is adamant that we be responsible with our time and our money, for these also become character issues.

What ONE area of stewardship do you feel like you need to grow in? Answer this part separately first.

Examples are: money; nutrition; exercise; sleep habits; eliminating time wasters; growing in my education and skills.

Now turn back together. As you compare answers, remember that your spouse may be very sensitive about this subject.

What ONE change can I make to get me on better footing in this area? Be as specific as possible.

Example: Instead of saying "lose weight," say, "I will start walking for twenty minutes after breakfast each day." Or instead of saying, "get out of debt," say, "I will start taking cash out at the beginning of each week and only spend that cash."

What ONE change can I make to support my spouse in the area that he/she wants to grow?
(Ask for their input here!)

For Parents

Add another layer to this: What character traits would you like most to see your children develop in the next year? List THREE.

Now compare notes and pray together. For each child, which ONE trait seems to resonate most?

What ONE thing do you need to most add to your life to help develop this trait?

Examples might be: eating dinner together as a family so we talk more; getting them involved in our church's children's ministry; having them write letters to our sponsored child; teaching them to tithe.

What ONE thing do you need to take away (or minimize) to prevent them going in the opposite direction?

Examples might be: turning off Wi-Fi at certain times of day; quitting some extracurricular activities; switching schools; limiting video game privileges.

What life skill do you want to concentrate on your children learning this year?

Examples could be: learning to clean up toys; learning to make a meal; learning to budget; learning to drive a car.

What is ONE new thing you can do to help them develop this skill?

What practically will this look like in your family?

Part II: The "Feel" of Our Family
Our Home Environment

The "feel" of every family is unique. Some homes radiate quiet and tranquility. Other families are chaotic, and live for spontaneity and fun. Others value music, or sports, or being the "hangout."

Take a few minutes and write down THREE words you believe describe the house/family environment that you want to have. Do this separately.

Compare notes. Can you see similarities? Talk through what these words mean to you. If you seem to have written down words that are polar opposites, talk about why it is that you like these words. What is it that you're longing for in your life? Let each person talk for two minutes without interruption, sharing their dreams.

As you listen to each other, do these words stir something in your own heart? Do your wife's dreams resonate? Do your husband's dreams cause something else to come to mind?

Try to focus now on one word. It may not be one that either of you wrote down; it may be one that you arrived at in discussing how you each see the house.

What ONE word will you work at nurturing as part of your family environment?

What can you implement TODAY to make your home feel that way?

Examples might be: If you want your house to be more musical, play a classical CD every dinnertime. If you want your house to feel more like a family and less like you're all on your own, decide to start eating dinner at a table together and get rid of TVs in people's bedrooms. If you want your family to feel more generous, pray about sponsoring a child. If you want your home to feel more welcoming, make sure the dining room and entryway are kept free of "stuff."

What can you work toward so that in ONE YEAR your family will look even more like your key word?

Examples might be: menu plan so you have meals at home more often; get rid of some outside commitments so you have time to pursue things that are more important; have the kids do chores so that the house stays more orderly; work toward getting out of debt so we aren't more stressed; have dad or mom home more.

In working to achieve this, what will SHE do to work toward this goal?

What will HE do to work toward this goal?

What will the CHILDREN (if you have any children) be responsible for as you work toward this goal?

Part III: Our Calling Together
How We Serve

Every family has a different role to play in what God is doing in the world. Some families will bless through music. Some will bless through hospitality. Some will teach, some will rescue, some will give. Some will serve in politics, some will fight for the unborn, and some will go overseas. Some will work toward a better environment and some toward a better neighborhood.

Thinking about your unique gifts as individuals, and your unique gifts as a family together, ask yourself (individually at first):

What role does our family have to play in God's kingdom? Think of THREE words that best describe this role.

Now compare notes. What similarities do you see? Pray through this together.

What ONE calling will we focus on as a family?

Remember, you can always focus on one thing now, and once it becomes more ingrained, or the children reach a different stage in life, focus on another thing!

Let's make it practical!

What ONE thing can we start doing TODAY to make this more of a reality in our home?

What ONE thing can we put in place so that we, as a family, will grow in this area of service and become more equipped for it?

Examples could be: asking an older couple involved in ministry to mentor you; volunteering at a pregnancy crisis center to learn more about what they do; having a new family over for dinner every week to be more hospitable; or even just starting to eat dinner together as a family so you feel more like a unit equipped for service!

Vision together: What do we want our family to look like in FIVE YEARS? In TEN YEARS? Use as many words as you can. Talk about this one together, not individually.

Ask yourselves honestly: Are we moving toward those goals, or away from them?

In what ways are we doing things right?

What things are getting in the way?

What can we do to get ourselves more on the road toward attaining those goals? Make this as practical and "doable" as possible.

That's it! I pray that this has proved useful as you have worked at turning your VALUES into a true VISION for your family!

It's great to do this exercise once a year because circumstances change and God is always talking to us about new things. So evaluate on a regular basis, and make sure that the way you live your life actually reflects your values—and leads your children toward them, too.

For Those Who Homeschool: Keeping Your Sanity as You Build Your Family

*I*f you're one of the more than half-a-million homeschooling moms, as I am, then you're involved in a very exciting adventure. When you made the decision to embark on this adventure, you likely did so with a touch of fear, a lot of love, and plenty of enthusiasm. Homeschooling has so much potential. It can help build a close-knit family and impart values to our kids while giving them a wonderful education. Too often, though, these dreams erode as our days become tense and unproductive. See if you can relate to this homeschooling day.

A Horror of a Day

Suzanne wakes up and realizes she's already overslept by fifteen minutes. Her toddler is crying, and the older kids have gone downstairs to watch a video. She can't get through the hall because all the laundry is piled in the middle of the floor (the laundry basket is still downstairs where she took it two days ago), and her kids' beds are not yet made.

Suzanne gathers some laundry in her arms and ventures downstairs, passing her kids along the way. She barks at them to get dressed, and while Tim reluctantly drags himself back upstairs, David, her eldest, and Michelle still sit glued to the tube. Johnny, her toddler, continues to cry.

After throwing in another load of laundry, she grabs Johnny, and she heads into the shower. She decides it's worth the hassle to have him with her if it will just stop his crying. Soon, however, soap is everywhere, including in his eyes, and the wailing has started again. To top it all off, Tim, her one obedient child, is now yelling that he can't find any clean underwear. Suzanne yells at him to go check the dryer, and asks him to tell his older siblings to go and get dressed, too.

By the time she emerges from the shower, gets dressed, and makes her bed (though Johnny is now bouncing on it and ruining all her hard work), her older children are still not dressed. This time Suzanne uses the really-angry voice, and they do make it upstairs.

Soon she's busy making breakfast. She asks the kids to go make their beds and clean their rooms while she fries the eggs. Hoping for some peace, she sits Johnny down with some Corn Flakes and a spoon while she grabs a cup of coffee and empties the dishwasher. Her peace is quickly shattered as her three children upstairs start fighting over who is cleaning up more. "Tim isn't cleaning, Mom! He's just sitting there playing with his Legos!"

Tim replies, "I already put away my stuff. That's your stuff!"

Michelle yells back, "But you were playing with it with me. You have to clean it, too!"

By now Suzanne's had enough. She heads upstairs, yells at them loudly enough to lift off the roof, and they get the room in some kind of order.

After breakfast she surveys the house. The kids' rooms are clean, but a pile of laundry still awaits her. The kitchen is a mess, the playroom is worse, and she's not sure when she last cleaned the bathroom. It's starting to get a little scary in there.

Suzanne decides she'll try to tackle it in between subjects. The kids sit down at their tables, and Tim announces he doesn't want to do math today. He wants to do art. To make the point, he grabs some crayons and proceeds to color. Suzanne looks with dismay at the six different subject workbooks piled up, all of which require half an hour of work. Several lessons require Suzanne to personally teach the kids, none of whom are currently quiet enough to listen. Michelle is kicking David's chair, and David is sticking his tongue out. Exasperated, she distributes the crayons to all and tells them to draw a picture while she cleans the bathroom. It's easier to deal with scum than to deal with these kids.

At the end of the day, the bathroom is cleaner, but the rest of the house is still a disaster. The kids didn't do three of their subjects. David would not sit still at math, and Michelle whined all through spelling. She just kept repeating that she couldn't do it. They were late to their piano lessons, which only increased Suzanne's humiliation. It was obvious the kids hadn't practiced, and she made some halfhearted excuse about maybe the flu was going around, and the kids were too tired.

By the time dinner rolled around, Suzanne was exhausted and ordered pizza. Another homeschooling day down the drain.

The Right Environment

When homeschooling goes badly, as it did for Suzanne, it's easy to fault homeschooling itself. Let's take a step back for a moment, and look at the problems Suzanne was facing. She was tired. Her kids didn't obey. The house was a mess. Her kids didn't want to learn. Her problems, in fact, had little to do with homeschooling. They're problems every parent has to deal with. But when we choose to homeschool as well, these problems become magnified. What some families can ignore or minimize, we can't, because we're home together so much more. All the potential problems in our families are laid bare and there's no escaping them. That doesn't mean that homeschooling is impossible! On the contrary, homeschooling gives us the push we need to address these issues that can no longer be swept under the rug.

Sometimes these issues are behavioral ones related to whether or not children listen and obey. Other problems are more organizational, including the perennial problem—mess. Often we forget that our homes can be more of a challenge simply because we're home so much more to mess them up.

I remember going to a friend's house for lunch one Sunday and being dismayed as I looked around her perfectly neat house. No clutter anywhere! Then Keith reminded me that she and her husband both worked long hours and the kids were in day care. They came home, ate, and went to bed. There simply wasn't time to mess up the house.

It's so crucial in homeschooling families that we organize our households, command respect from our kids, and find time to renew ourselves. If we can do this, not only will school go well, we'll also find that our families can become an amazing place of refuge for us. How do we make this transformation? First, we need the right environment for homeschooling:

An Organized Household. You need to be able to find crayons, markers, paper, books, or whatever when you need them, and you'll need a clean surface to work on.

Room for Imagination. Homeschoolers don't necessarily need immaculate homes. In fact, homes should be filled with books to nurture the imagination, containing games that inspire learning, and science projects that invite exploring! But these things all need a place to be put when kids are finished with them, if only to ensure they don't get broken, lost, or torn.

Relaxed Time for Learning. Finally, kids need to learn in a relaxed environment. No one learns well when someone is standing over them yelling, trying to get through a difficult math lesson quickly because there is just too much to get done that day. You need to have time devoted exclusively to schooling. Then your kids will know that at that moment they are your most important priority.

All of this, like those stone fences I mentioned earlier, takes some work, but the payoffs are wonderful. Let's look at how we can accomplish this.

Get Organized

First and foremost, you need to get organized. This means, much as it goes against many of our personality types, a schedule.

Clean to a Schedule

That schedule begins first thing in the morning. I've asked many successful homeschooling families how they handle cleaning up. Here's what almost all of them said: "We do it before school, usually before 9 AM." When my girls were younger, and homeschooling was entirely hands-on (as opposed to the high school years, which are far more independent), we started waking up at 7, which was a stretch for me. That way we were finished with breakfast and cleaning our own rooms (even mine!) by 8, and then we could spend forty-five minutes on the house. I had a four-week schedule, similar to the one I suggested in chapter 3, where everything was cleaned according to a plan. Once my daily allotment was done, I could hang up my mop and my dust rag. At 8:45, we all read our Bibles before we began school. I felt so organized!

We also did another big tidy-up before dinner, but the rest of the day I had free to devote to other things. This worked because the girls were equally involved in the cleaning. One morning, while I cleaned the kitchen, they did our main bathroom. The next day, they'll clean all the mirrors and windows on our main floor while I mop and vacuum. They received an allowance, which they loved to spend, and I rarely heard complaints from them. I do not allow them to play until all this is done. It became a natural part of our routine, and it worked well. And when my oldest left home, she had saved so much of her allowance she had enough for two years of tuition!

Run Errands to a Schedule

The other thing we need to get organized is running errands. Every week there are things we must do, like running to the hardware store, scheduling a doctor's appointment, going to the bank, picking up something at the mall, and, of course, grocery shopping. This is so much easier if you can do it all at once! So I picked one day a week for errands. All dentist's appointments, doctor's appointments (except emergencies, obviously), car tune-ups, or anything else were always scheduled on that day.

This also necessitated planning all meals for the week ahead of time so that I only had to venture to the grocery store once a week. I tended to buy fresh vegetables and eat them at the beginning of the week, using other things for lunches and dinners later in the week. For instance, I'd have sandwiches for a few days after grocery shopping, and macaroni and cheese with some fruit a few days later.

All these errands didn't disrupt our schooling because we have arranged the schedule to be only four days a week. This allowed a free day for errands, outside lessons, going to the park, going on a field trip, getting together with homeschooling friends, or anything else we could dream of.

Organize Your School

Our household schedules are not the only ones that need organizing. Our school schedules, too, need to be organized. Perhaps you want to allow the kids a play break, like recess, after a few subjects. By all means do so, but don't let them get that play break until those subjects are finished. If the kids are dawdling and you decide to let them go in the hopes that they will come back more ready to work, this may backfire on you.

Scheduling subjects doesn't necessarily mean scheduling exact times. At our house, sometimes we homeschooled in the mornings, sometimes in the afternoons, and sometimes in the middle of the day, depending on the amount of time various lessons take and homeschooling association activities. For instance, during the elementary years I knew I needed about two and a half hours altogether, with the first twenty minutes devoted to Bible, and the next half hour devoted to phonics, spelling, and composition. If I knew what I needed to teach and how much emphasis to give each subject, it wouldn't matter whether I start at 9, 11, or 1. It will still all get done.

The other big organization challenge for our school day is corralling the little ones. Nothing disrupts your homeschooled kids more than having a little sibling yelling, grabbing, singing, or otherwise trying (and probably succeeding) to distract them. There's plenty available on the Internet on the subject of amusing toddlers while you school, but it goes without saying that you need a plan. Perhaps they can have a special box of toys that only comes out at school time, or their own activities so they can do school, too. Maybe it's worth beginning school fifteen minutes later each day simply to organize things for your toddler to do. If you can amuse him or her, your day will go much more smoothly.

Use the Right Teaching Method

Another way to reduce stress is to make sure you adopt a teaching method that works for your personality type, your schedule, the number of children you have, and, of course, their learning styles. Homeschooling catalogs are full of a variety of curriculum choices, from those that utilize the strict "half-hour-a-workbook" session to those that use unit studies, or even unschooling. What is right for you will depend on your philosophy of education, your time, and your preferences. I have talked to many homeschoolers who have felt discouraged because their program was so regimented and boring, and others who feared they weren't being regimented enough.

Having a regimented curriculum does have some benefits. There's little planning involved on your part, so you can dive into teaching with little preparation. Often there's a happy medium, such as the unit study approach, which tells you everything you need and what to do without relying on workbooks. Nevertheless, you'll have to plan ahead to make sure you have the right materials on the right day. If organizing and planning materials is part of the fun for you—as it is for Keith and me—you may choose no particular curriculum at all, so that you can put it together yourself.

But whatever you do, don't choose a curriculum because it works great for that family with seven kids, or because you think that's what homeschooling should be. Join a homeschooling association, go online, or call some curriculum publishers and ask for advice. There's so much out there; choose something that works with your schedule, that you find interesting, and that your kids will do willingly.

Provide Escapes

If you and your kids are cooped up all day, even if you're doing something fun, you're going to start to go a little stir-crazy. Plan escapes for all of you. Go for a quick bike ride or a walk around the block. Go to a park, visit some friends, or invite some over. If you have transportation (and some money!) schedule music lessons, gymnastics lessons, or soccer practices.

Perhaps one of the best benefits of homeschooling is the opportunity for quick, inexpensive field trips. Call up your fire station, a local factory, a recycling plant, a trucking company, or a dairy. Many of these would be happy to have you visit, and it doesn't have to take up too much of your day. Explore nearby wetlands; take a walk in the forest; or trek, armed with a net, to a nearby pond. Planning little educational escapes can be fun for the kids, help them feel connected to the community, and invigorate them to do school again once you get home.

Foster Respect

Perhaps nowhere is the need for kids to respect their parent more evident than when that parent is the teacher, too. If your children don't listen to you, getting them to concentrate on math, spelling, or writing a composition will be a nightmare. It will drain you, it will frustrate them, and it will confound the efforts of any siblings who are trying to work at the same time.

You simply must foster respect. Your kids have to know consequences so that they push the limits only occasionally. Try setting rules for school-related behavior. For instance, we didn't allow our daughters to whine or to say, "I can't do this!" If they did, they went to their beds to lie down (without a book or toy) because they were obviously too tired. They soon willingly returned! Have zero tolerance for anything that sounds or feels disrespectful.

Ask your spouse to support you in this bid to command their respect. How he treats you often determines how the children treat you. If your husband lets the kids know it is unacceptable to talk back to their mother, they will listen. After all, would they treat their teacher in school that way? Obviously not, so they should not treat you that way, either.

Renew Yourself

Finally, you need some time to renew yourself. Many of us choose to homeschool because our kids give us joy. We may not even feel like we particularly need a break from them. But whether we feel it or not, time to ourselves, to plan, to pray, to dream, or just to do nothing, is vital.

Luckily, as homeschoolers, we know more about expanding our interests than your average person does. We're used to researching new subject areas, going to the library, checking out the community college courses, or scouring community papers for interesting lectures. Usually we do this to find educational opportunities, but we can also do it to find renewal opportunities for ourselves.

Joining homeschooling associations and meeting other moms in our area who homeschool, can also renew us. Getting together and comparing notes can be useful, comforting, and exciting as we learn new tips and realize we're all in the same boat!

Finally, give your husband some time, too. As homeschooling families, the children are almost always included in everything we do. Go away for a weekend once a year, take dates occasionally, or reserve fifteen to twenty minutes a night just to talk, with your door shut, and the kids banished. Nurture your marriage relationship, so that you have the strength to teach your kids.

Homeschoolers have already decided to prioritize their kids above all else. But that doesn't guarantee a successful homeschooling experience or a peaceful home life. You'll need organization, diligence, a firm hand at disciplining, and lots of creativity. As you build a successful homeschool, you'll also be building a successful family. It's a big order, but you can do it with a little planning and a big dose of God's help!

Notes

Chapter 1: Diagnosis: Stress

1. Women's Health Sciences Center, Women's Health Study, Toronto, Ontario, 1998.

2. Centers for Disease Control and Prevention, "QuickStats: Percentage of Adults Who Often Felt Very Tired or Exhausted in the Past 3 Months, by Sex and Age Group–National Health Interview Survey, United States, 2010–2011," *Morbidity and Mortality Weekly Report* 62, no. 14 (April 12, 2013), 275.

3. Martha Rhodes, "Tips to Tackle Exhaustion," ABC News Women's Health, April 29, 2012, http://abcnews.go.com/Health/Wellness/tips-tackle-exhaustion/story?id=16228332.

4. David Futtrelle, "Closing the Chore Gap." Time Magazine Business & Money, December 21, 2012, http://business.time.com/2012/12/21/closing-the-chore-gap/.

5. Wendy Wang, "Parents' Time with Kids More Rewarding Than Paid Work—and More Exhausting." PewResearch Social and Demographic Trends, October 8, 2013, http://www.pewsocialtrends.org/2013/10/08/parents-time-with-kids-more-rewarding-than-paid-work-and-more-exhausting/.

6. Amanda Hess, "Parents Rate Child Care as 'Exhausting' and 'Meaningful.' Work? Not Meaningful," The XX Factor, *Slate*, October 10, 2013, http://www.slate.com/blogs/xx_factor/2013/10/10/pew_study_on_modern_american_family_moms_still_do_more_childcare.html.

7. Quoted by Jane Louise Boursaw, "Work Daze," *Sonoma County Independent*, August 1999, http://www.metroactive.com/papers/sonoma/08.12.99/work-9932.html.

8. From www.momsnetwork.com, accessed February 24, 2003, http://www.montessori.org/Resources/Library/Parents/whatilearned.htm.

9. "Canadian Attitudes on the Family," *Focus on the Family Canada*, June 2002, http://www.imfcanada.org/sites/default/files/Canadian%20Attitudes %20on%20the%20Family.pdf.

10. See, for instance, Stephen Covey, *The Seven Habits of Highly Effective People: Powerful Lessons in Personal Change* (New York: Simon & Schuster, 1989).

11. Marilyn Ferguson cited in ibid., 60–61.

Chapter 2: One Step Forward, Two Steps Back

1. Of course, the exodus off the farm started much earlier than this, but it wasn't until the early twentieth century when half of all families lived off of farms. So in the late 1800s, life for most Americans still meant the family farm.

2. Stanly Lebergott, *The American Economy: Income, Wealth, and Want* (Princeton, NJ: Princeton University Press, 1976), 508.

3. Steve Hargreaves, "15% of Americans Living in Poverty," *CNN Money*, September 17, 2013, http://money.cnn.com/2013/09/17/news/economy /poverty-income/.

4. Annenberg Public Policy Center, Media in the Home 2000, cited by TV Free Turnoff Network, Fact Sheet, 2001.

Chapter 3: This Aint My Mama's House!

1. C. S. Lewis, *Mere Christianity*, final lines of chapter 4.

2. Mimi Wilson and Mary Beth Lagerborg, *Once-a-Month Cooking: A Proven System for Spending Less Time in the Kitchen and Enjoying Delicious, Homemade Meals Every Day* (New York: St. Martin's Press, 1986).

3. Kathy Peel, *The Family Manager* (Nashville, TN: W. Publishing Group, 1996).

Chapter 4: Balancing Tipped Scales

1. See Susan Wittig Albert, *A Work of Her Own: A Woman's Guide to Creating a Right Livelihood* (New York: G. P. Putnam's Sons, 1992).

2. Tony Campolo, *Twenty Hot Potatoes Christians Are Afraid to Touch* (Dallas: Word, 1998), 29.

3. Stephen Covey, *The Seven Habits of Highly Effective People: Powerful Lessons in Personal Change* (New York: Simon & Schuster, 1989), 151.

4. See the story of Gordon MacDonald in "Beyond Burnout" by Richelle Wiseman, *Faith Today*, May–June 1998, 30, available at http://www.christianity.ca/page.aspx?pid=11406.

Chapter 5: Relationship U-Turns

1. Cynthia S. Smith, *The Seven Levels of Marriage: Expectations Versus Reality* (Secaucus, NJ: Lyle Stuart, 1986), 14.

2. Susan Page, *Now That I'm Married, Why Isn't Everything Perfect?* (New York: Dell, 1994), 8.

3. Gay C. Kitson, *Portrait of Divorce: Adjustment to Marital Breakdown* (New York: Guilford Press, 1992), 65.

4. Linda J. Waite, Don Browning, William J. Doherty, Maggie Gallagher, Ye Luo, and Scott M. Stanley, *Does Divorce Make People Happy? Findings from a Study of Unhappy Marriages* (New York: Institute for American Values, 2002). http://americanvalues.org/catalog/pdfs/does_divorce_make_people_happy.pdf.

5. One of the best books dealing with this phenomenon is Robin Norwood's *Women Who Love Too Much: When You Keep Wishing and Hoping He'll Change* (New York: Simon & Schuster, 1985). Though it is not a Christian book, she seems sympathetic to religious views, and I think the conclusions are just as relevant for women in the church as for those outside of it.

6. Henry Cloud, "Getting Results," Cloud-Townsend Resources, July 27, 2000, http://www.cloudtownsend.com/getting-results/.

7. This is not to say that God did not in some way "curse" people to subsequent generations, only that one of the ways in which such a curse may be felt is in the natural laws of our psychological makeup that God created.

8. Mary Stewart Van Leeuwen, *Gender and Grace: Love, Work and Parenting in a Changing World* (Downers Grove, IL: InterVarsity, 1990).

9. Maxine Hancock, *Creative, Confident Children* (Wheaton, IL: Harold Shaw, 1992).

10. For a more detailed discussion of this "reaping and sowing" principle, see Henry Cloud and John Townsend, *Boundaries: When to Say Yes, How to Say No to Take Control of Your Life* (Grand Rapids: Zondervan, 1992), 84–86.

11. Norwood, *Women Who Love Too Much*, 177.

Chapter 6: The Family That Cleans Together

1. Scott Coltrane, *Family Man: Fatherhood, Housework and Gender Equity* (New York: Oxford University Press, 1996), 7.

2. University of Cambridge, "Charting Gender's 'Incomplete Revolution,'" Research News, June 27, 2012, http://www.cam.ac.uk/research/news /charting-genders-incomplete-revolution.

3. Carol Cassell, *Tender Bargaining: Negotiating an Equal Partnership with the Man You Love* (Los Angeles: Jack Arenstein, 1993), 11.

4. Quoted in ibid., 160.

5. Ibid.

6. See John Gray, *Men Are from Mars, Women Are from Venus: The Classic Guide to Understanding the Opposite Sex* (New York: HarperCollins, 1992), 266.

7. Harriet Goldhor Lerner, *Dance of Anger: A Woman's Guide to Changing the Patterns of Intimate Relationships* (New York: Harper & Row, 1985), 33.

8. Gray, *Men Are from Mars, Women Are from Venus*, 56.

9. This is a point that John Gray makes at length in his book. And from everyone I've talked to, and observing men in action, I think he's absolutely right!

10. Gray, *Men Are from Mars, Women Are from Venus*, 259.

11. Ibid., 56.

12. Lerner, *Dance of Anger*, 137.

Chapter 7: Don't Just Sit There—Do Something!

1. Geri Scazzero, *The Emotionally Healthy Woman: Eight Things You Have to Quit to Change Your Life* (Grand Rapids: Zondervan, 2013), 160.

2. Neale S. Godfrey with Tad Richards, *A Penny Saved: Teaching Your Children the Values and Life Skills They Will Need to Live in the Real World* (New York: Simon & Schuster, 1996).

3. Reginald Bibby and Donald Posterski, *Teen Trends: A Nation in Motion* (Toronto: Stoddart, 1992), 150.

4. Michele Weiner Davis, *Divorce Busting* (New York: Summit Books, 1992), 140.

5. Scazzero, *The Emotionally Healthy Woman*, 160.

6. Sue Careless, "Burnout: Who's at Risk?" *Faith Today*, May–June 1998, 32.

Chapter 8: Kids Spell Love T-I-M-E

1. Dr. Laura Schlessinger, *How Could You Do That? The Abdication of Character, Courage and Conscience* (New York: HarperCollins, 1996), 89.

2. Charmaine Crouse Yoest, "Parents at Home: Still the Silent Majority," *Family Policy*, March 1998. She does a very good overview of all the major longitudinal and large-scale studies on day care.

3. Pooja S. Tandon, Chuan Zhou, Paula Lozano, and Dimitri Christakis, "Preschoolers' Total Daily Screen Time at Home and by Type of Child Care," *Journal of Pediatrics* 158, no. 2 (February 2011), doi: 10.1016/j.peds.2010.08.005.

4. American Academy of Pediatrics, "Media and Children" under AAP Health Initiatives, accessed March 25, 2014, http://www.aap.org/en-us/advocacy-and-policy/aap-health-initiatives/pages/media-and-children.aspx.

5. National Institute on Media and the Family, 1999, cited in Facts and Figures About Our TV Habit, TV Turnoff Network, 2002, accessed March 22, 2002, www.tvturnoff.org/factsheets.htm.

6. David Popenoe, *Life Without Father: Compelling New Evidence That Fatherhood and Marriage Are Indispensable for the Good of Children and Society* (New York: Simon & Schuster, 1996), 143.

7. Floyd McClung, *Living on the Devil's Doorstep: From Kabul to Amsterdam* (Dallas: Word, 1999).

Chapter 9: Bringing Your Wallet Under God's Control

1. See Kay Arthur, *Lord, Heal My Hurts* (Portland, OR: Multnomah, 1989) for a discussion of this. Her chapters on "Letting Your Mind Be Renewed" and "Your Mind: The Battlefield" are especially relevant.

2. Janet Luhr, *The Simple Living Guide* (New York: Broadway Books, 1997).

3. Meghan Casserly, "Is Opting-Out the New American Dream for Working Women?" ForbesWomen, September 12, 2012, http://www.forbes.com/sites/meghancasserly/2012/09/12/is-opting-out-the-new-american-dream-for-working-women/.

4. Charmaine Crouse Yoest, "Parents at Home: Still the Silent Majority," *Family Policy*, March 1998, 2.

5. Taken from ibid., 6.

6. Jay Belsky, "Parental and Nonparental Child Care and Children's Socio-emotional Development: A Decade in Review," *Journal of Marriage and Family* 52, no. 4 (November 1990), 895.

7. Mary Eberstadt, "Home-Alone America," *Policy Review*, June 1, 2001, http://www.hoover.org/publications/policy-review/article/6610.

8. An excellent book on this subject is by Joseph R. Dominguez and Vicki Robin, *Your Money or Your Life: Nine Steps to Transforming Your Relationship with Money and Achieving Financial Independence* (New York: Penguin Books, 1999).

9. Marjorie Williams, "Mommy at Her Desk," April 25, 2001, http://www.washingtonpost.com/wp-dyn/articles/A61332-2001Apr24.html.

10. This trend was exacerbated by contraception and abortion, which also offered sex without pregnancy. Now, if a woman got pregnant, it was effectively her fault and he didn't need to take responsibility for it. He was responsibility-free in every way.

11. See William J. Bennett, *The Broken Hearth: Revising the Moral Collapse of the American Family* (New York: Doubleday, 2001), for an explanation of this.

Chapter 10: In the Mood

1. From "The Experiment" by Catherine Marshall, retold by Marilyn K. McAuley in *Stories for the Heart: 110 Stories to Encourage Your Soul*, comp. Alice Gray (Sisters, OR: Multnomah, 1996), 74.